Isabel Salema Morgado

Facts, lies and opinions

Isabel Salema Morgado

Facts, lies and opinions

Ethical-political discourse and its legitimisation criteria

ScienciaScripts

Cover image: Provided by the author

This book is a translation from the original published under ISBN 978-3-330-19997-2.

Publisher:
Sciencia Scripts
is a trademark of
Dodo Books Indian Ocean Ltd. and OmniScriptum S.R.L publishing group

120 High Road, East Finchley, London, N2 9ED, United Kingdom
Str. Armeneasca 28/1, office 1, Chisinau MD-2012, Republic of Moldova, Europe
Printed at: see last page
ISBN: 978-620-8-26660-8

Index

1 The truth of the matter

An excursus on the "FactCheck" service in political journalism[1]

In 1968, in her text *Truth and Politics,* Hannah Arendt wrote that "Facts and events are infinitely more fragile than the axioms, discoveries and theories - even the most wildly speculative - produced by the human spirit; (...) Once lost, no rational effort can bring them back."[2] Only someone who lived, thought and wrote in a time markedly dominated by the will and the power to distort facts could make a statement like that. A time marked by the massive presence of propaganda and the dominance of public relations principles in political and social discourse, in public presentation. A time in which the presentation of the object (affirming the possibility of immediate knowledge of it) is overestimated in relation to the reality of that object, as David Beetham reinforces.[3] A fact is a concept which indicates an event that has already occurred or something that is considered to have been done. In language, we can highlight the presence of linguistic facts whenever we consider a speech act to have been consummated, which can then be analyzed in terms of its content.

For example: the statement by the then Republican candidate for president of the United States, George H.W. Bush in 1988, "Read my lips: no new taxes". This public pledge not to raise taxes if elected to the presidency would have had a significant impact on the voting decision of the Republican voters who elected him and which was broken while he was in office, as political and economic circumstances did not allow him to keep his promise. In other words, the electoral promise transformed into a declarative sentence, which affirms a fact, into an assertion, gained truth value. This is an example of how the effect of these phrases can help win elections, if it connotes the possibility of being true, and lose them, when the facts come into question, making these phrases false.

It is true that Western philosophers, from classical antiquity onwards, have warned of the fragile nature of events as a source of value in describing or valuing human action, but for different reasons from those that led Arendt to do so. Arendt believed that it was impossible for language to stick to its descriptive function of facts in order to provide

---

Paper presented at the University of Beira Interior, as part of the II Conference on Communication and Politics. Research work funded by the Foundation for Science and Technology and institutional support by the Nova University of Lisbon. The article was updated in June 2017.

[2] Hannah Arendt (1967), *Verdade e Politica*, transl. Manuel Alberto, Lisbon, Relogio d'Agua, 1995, p. 15.

[3] David Beetham (1991), *The Legitimation of Power,* Hampshire, Palgrave, 1991, p. 9.

access to their truth, since due to their mutable nature - social phenomena cannot be understood/predicted by means of a general law - facts would not constitute a sure criterion of the stability and universality that the question of truth requires as its foundation; rational and philosophical truth. This is a demand for truth that only a dialectical investigation conducted by human reason could meet.[4] At the time, rational truth and the truth of facts did not have the same value, because this truth was the one that concerned the material and social world, the other the one that could be manifested through thought, the essence of what remains in spite of the physical change of the reality that appears to us.

Arendt is not concerned with the question of the diversity of opinions that exist in society, she is not disturbed by the multiplicity of perspectives on a given phenomenon, what interests her is identifying the process found by each person to legitimize and defend these opinions, according to the use of the strict criterion of the concept "truth of fact" as a way of distinguishing truth from lies. The author advocates respecting the truth of the matter, since facts are the material of opinions,[5] and their truth is that which can be attested to "by the eyes of the body, not by the eyes of the spirit",[6] which allows the least manipulated approximation to reality possible.

Let's bear in mind: the opposite of the truth of the matter is not opinion, or one more opinion, but lies.[7] Both truth and opinion are not more evident than each other, since they depend equally on the strength of the testimonies. There is no *per se* evidence of the truth of the matter, because there is no force emanating from it that would constrain the pronouncement of the truth. What concerns her, then, is the question of the nature of the action taken by the holders of opinion as a means of exercising or obtaining power, i.e. politicians, in making the truth of fact, in the realm of human affairs, acceptable or recognizable as just another opinion among others. A perspective on a given object or action that is just as acceptable, or even less acceptable, as the particular interest defines

---

4 Heraclitus and his disciple Cratylus taught how everything flows in physical nature. The Sophists taught with Protagoras that "Man is the measure of all things". These principles relativized knowledge about reality, offering it as passive! to be interpreted in opposite ways, although both perfectly defensible. This conclusion conquered political reality and transformed the very conception of the state in Athens, for example, when the nobles, divided into parties - the oligarchs and the democrats - found themselves having to win over the opinions of the people to their cause as a result of an internal factional struggle for power after the death of Pericles. See Werner Jaeger, *The Paideia,* transl. Artur M. Parreira, Lisbon, Aster, 1979:311 to 357.
The problem of communicating power lies in the type of communication that politicians choose and use to persuade or convince their fellow citizens to support their side. In other words, why does the conflict between truth and politics remain open?

5 Hannah Arendt (1967), p. 24.

6 Id., p.23.

7 Id., p. 52.

it, than any other opinion. This often occurs and is particularly evident whenever the truth of the matter is opposed to the interests or pleasures of those with the power to produce and disseminate opinion, when attempts are made to level the truth of the matter to the dominance of opinion production.

It seems that we are facing a paradox: on the one hand we understand the historical and socially created nature of the event that is called a fact, but on the other hand we evoke the existence of a truth of fact as a reality/creed that allows us to describe the reality of things as they are. This ambiguity in the definition of the term is better understood, although this ambiguity does not determine its nature, if we understand the example that Arendt, quoting the French physician and politician Georges Clemenceau, gave us, ªby saying that while we can discuss at length and with different interlocutors taking different positions on the reasons that led to the outbreak of World War I, we can no longer say, as a matter of opinion, that it was Belgium that invaded Germany.[8]

Arendt understood very well the duality present in her object of study, but she didn't let this epistemological problem serve as an obstacle to her thesis in which she argued that, in the relationship with political power, facts present themselves as a phenomenon of greater stability because they are more resistant against, and in relation to, the transient interests of the individuals who come together to exercise power. From this point of view, politicians should be aware that facts should not be taken as the result of a process that is indifferent or constrained by the will of human beings, nor should they be understood as material that can be denied, without major consequences for the relationships of trust established between [9] rulers and ruled in representative democracies.

If the author believes that the nature of fact belongs to the same domain as that of opinion, because both depend on evidence presented by witnesses and both manifest themselves in the discourses used to convince others, she nevertheless tries to explain the distinct nature of these phenomena. It is true that the author recognizes that the evidence of the fact, its assertiveness, is not given by itself once and for all, nor is there any guarantee outside or superior to that of its discursive manifestation that guarantees its truth. Arendt does not have a positivist awareness of de facto reality. For her, there is no possibility of making an immediate and uncritical appropriation of reality, since she realizes that facts and events are always presented in thought as a reality mediated by the language of human beings, by their social interactions.

---

8 Id., p. 25.

But philosophy also knows that there are factors in human behavior that can be classified as impartial and tending towards objectivity. There are ways of overvaluing this mechanism, which consists of highlighting things, promoting an action of detachment of the subject from the object that is enunciated, and which is accepted and recognized by the other subjects in interaction. There are ways of exalting this objectivity or concealing it in the language used to communicate with one's peers. Arendt considers these phenomena of concealment/unveiling in the discourse of the reality of things to be a passion of Western human intellect. The example she gives is that of the classical authors Homer and Hesiod. The former because, for the first time in history, a storyteller sought to narrate both the successes and defeats of the victors and the vanquished. The latter, not being a poet, presents himself as a keeper of the memory of the actions undertaken by the peoples at the time, the Greeks and the barbarians, in order to give a broad perspective on the events, avoiding the temptation to describe and praise exclusively the achievements of his people.[9][10]

These authors would have brought to human history a new perspective on reality, a different positioning of the narrator in relation to the historical object narrated, which can be summed up as the possibility for those in the position of judge or narrator of an event to suspend the egocentric act of considering only their personal interests, or those of their group, above those of everyone else when making the final assessment or narration of an event. By freeing themselves from exclusively personal considerations in the judgments they make, each author is putting the abstract concept of impartiality into practice.[11]

There are many gnosiological and epistemological problems arising from this intellectual exercise, but the notion that one can judge without taking sides, with impartiality, came to be at the basis of the idea of producing scientific knowledge about reality, of the possibility of enunciating a general law for natural phenomena.[12]
In 1973 Karl-Otto Apel made us understand how the demand for the certification of a fact is a sign that human beings have managed to discover that it is in language, and

[9] Id., p. 53.
[10] Id., p. 58.
[11] Id., p. 57.
[12] Daniel Cornu, in his book, *Jornalismo e Verdade (Journalism and Truth),* published in Portuguese by the Piaget Institute in 1999, refers to the emergence of the notion of objectivity in modern times, which is linked to the autonomy of scientific knowledge in relation to philosophical knowledge which, at the end of the 18th century, advocated the use of observation and experimentation as a method of study in order to achieve a positivist understanding of reality. He tells us that *the Grand Larrousse de la Langue Francaise* and the *Robert* indicate that 1803 was the year in which the notion appeared. But, as Arendt explained to us, Herodotus, even without presenting the concept, had already enunciated the reality that would be defined by the term "objectivity".

through it, that the question of examining the correctness of a fact can evolve.[13] The appropriation of the reality of a fact is made through the meaning that this fact has for the person or the community, and this can be explored either through logical intellectual pondering, judging and discussing it (thought experiments), or by carrying out a series of practical experiments and observations that verify the meaning of sentences through extra-linguistic facts.

Jurgen Habermas works along the same lines when he subscribes to the Appelian theory that a fact is a linguistic reality that depends on the inter-personal recognition of the community of speakers. Not that these authors defend the non-existence of a material world, a world whose occurrence beyond what is capable of being linguistically mediated would be denied, what they understand is that this world can only be accessed by what is manifested in language. And in language, in the use of propositions that express judgments about events, the question of truth value is raised and supports the verification, by adequacy, of the content of the statement with the reality affirmed or denied.

Although, as we have learned from the philosophers of communication, a speech act is not restricted to its propositional domain, because the meaning of an utterance is not equivalent to its propositional meaning, since there is also an illocutionary force, which allows us to say that a speech act is not limited to recording the relationship between the assertoric phrase describing the world and the things described in that world, but is also an act that provokes a certain effect in the listeners, which depends on whether they understand the manifestation/speech, whether they recognize it, and whether they accept or reject its meaning. [14] In other words, the meaning of what is said, its acceptance, is broader than the question of truth, although without truth, truth as correspondent or verification, there is no meaning in language either.

Arendt is also aware that the person who tells the truth in fact is still a "storyteller", a being who tries to reconcile thought and reality[15] , which is why, as the author tells us, the proof of facts does not go beyond the realm of analyzing information, which can be obtained through testimonies, found in archives, documents or monuments.[16] A fact can be manipulated to the extent that you can easily coerce people into giving false

---

13 Karl-Otto Apel (1973), "Language and truth...", in *Transformation of Philosophy,* Vol.1, transl. Soethe, Sao Paulo, ed. Loyola, 2000:163-196.

14 Jurgen Habermas (1976), "What is universal pragmatics?", in Maeve Cooke (ed.), *On the Pragmatics of Communication,* Cambridge, Polity, 1998.

15 Id., p.57.

16 Id., pp. 24 and 31.

testimony, just as you can make archives, documents and even monuments disappear.[17] All dictatorial or authoritarian political powers do this more or less explicitly.

The work of preserving a de facto truth in the human sciences is all the more delicate when we realize how it is possible for those in power in society to select, defend and disseminate the events that interest them by rewriting history. And even more seriously, as Arendt realized, it's not that those who can rewrite history do so with the explicit intention of deceiving others in order to obtain benefits, or in order to make them adhere to their visions in the name of some ideal, by instrumentalizing communication, but that they deceive themselves into believing that the image they propagate is really the correct image of reality. [18]

Arendt's concern about attacks on the factual material itself[19] is common to all those in journalism, or in the academies of human and social studies, who evoke the need for a separation between the sphere of activity and influence of those in power, and those who are working on the analysis or presentation of news related to the facts that result from the discursive or executive action of that power.

In order for a factual truth to be accepted, its issuer needs to be recognized by his interlocutors as an independent actor, unrelated to the interests of the established powers illegitimately interested in controlling all information. Only in this way will it present itself as an authority figure that will impose itself against anyone who contradicts its proposals.

This is the sense of independence that we want to preserve in order to guarantee the objectivity and impartiality of what we say, when we create a mechanism that preserves the truth of the matter from the attacks with which the powers that be, particularly the political powers, might seek to reject it. But this issue is not without its problems, because it is not consensually accepted by all those interested in this field. And while it is true that it is in the sense of those who defend the existence of truths of fact that we can understand the creation of the deontological code for journalists[20] , and as far as its

[17] The author gives several examples in her book. We can recall the recent event of the destruction of the archaeological city of Palmyra in Syria in 2016 by the Islamic extremists of ISIS, or 2001, when in Afghanistan the "Taliban", then in power, ordered the destruction of the Giant Buddhas carved out of the desert rock in the Bamyan region.

[18] *Id.*, "(...) in fully democratic conditions, deception without self-deception is almost impossible.", p.49.

[19] Id., p.25.

[20] Because surprisingly academies, teachers in general, don't seem to have had the need/opportunity so far to create their own code. It would be interesting to know the reasons for this. Is it fundamentally because it is not perceived as a liberal profession?

legal character is concerned,[21] has an *item* that emphasizes the role of the journalist as one who respects the truth of what he or she describes, taking the fact of being objective as truth, it is also true that there is a very strong current that considers that "objectivity does not exist."

As Daniel Cornu clearly and accessibly writes in his book *Journalism and Truth*, it is above all in the Anglo-Saxon journalistic tradition that we are taught to rigorously separate what belongs to the sphere of information technology from what belongs to the field of commentary,[22] French-influenced journalism takes a more radical refusal to consider the existence of objective journalistic work, preferring to replace the concept of work that aims to be objective with work that aims to be honest. [23] However, the author also warns us against easily cataloguing this ethical and methodological position, which argues that journalists should focus above all on reporting facts, as if it were "Anglo-Saxon naivety".

While it's correct to say that the reality we have access to is an interpreted reality, since even when we observe it, we can't assume that we're dealing with a "raw fact", because from the outset we're selecting it, qualifying it and working it through our socially inherited perceptions and cognitive faculties, it is also true to say that objectivity is the search for the accuracy of a fact that is verifiable, that is, validated by a wide range of people who will testify to its appropriateness - the professional community or, at the end of the day, the community of readers best equipped to research and assess the degree of accuracy and truthfulness in the reports.[24]

Daniel Cornu sums up the problematic nature of this issue exceptionally well when he writes: "Journalistic objectivity, it should be noted, navigates between the illusion of a sacralization of the facts, which would lead to the elimination of the journalist as a subject, and the risk of an interpretation that abstracts or limits them."[25] This is why journalists, in their relationship with political power, should try to have sufficient distance from their object of analysis (in most cases the object in question will be the speeches of political actors), knowing in advance that political power has the capacity,

---

[21] In addition to codifying the conditions of employment and the rules governing the exercise of the profession, the codes also list the main duties of a journalist, one of which is present across all the codes and formalizes the requirement to respect the truth of the information. Many strategies have been used to achieve this mission, from the creation of national press councils, to observatories, to the creation of the ombudsman in some newspapers.

Daniel Cornu (1994), *Jornalismo e Verdade,* transl. Dorindo Carvalho, Lisbon, Inst. Piaget, 1999, p. 327.

Id., p. 328.

Id., p. 357.

Id., p. 341.

even if it is not exercised with authoritarianism, to impose analytical grids (to propose behavioral rules for the various social systems) on the reality that best suits its immediate interests.

If journalism considers that this is a false question, that it is not the job of its professionals to work with methods that refer to the scientific illusion, and that the relationship between scientists and the truth of the matter should remain at the level of an honest exposition of the events described in a linguistic domain that is widely understood, isn't it agreeing to uncritically convey the ideology of the ruling power? Aren't we confusing the right to make mistakes, which derives from any work carried out honestly, with the right to lie, which is, in fact, what opposes the denial of a factual truth?

In recent years, a type of association has emerged in the public sphere with an intervention that parallels that of the traditional media, because its aim is to inform the public, but at the same time it is a community service whose members dedicate themselves to an activity carried out with purpose and with a methodological requirement analogous to that of a scientist describing facts. In this specific case, the specific and delimited object of the reality under investigation is represented by the content of what is announced in speeches, interviews and press releases by politicians. And, more specifically in the service carried out in the United States, to analyze the content of paid political advertisements. This activity takes place mainly during election campaigns, but not only.

Knowing that the facts don't speak for themselves, isn't this Anglo-Saxon academic or journalistic activity an illusion?

One of the theoretical references for this area is the author Kathleen Hall Jamieson. She argues that political discourse inevitably refers to a reality that presupposes a set of verifiable facts, and that this verification is the first test of any political proposal. And he gives several lessons on how this test can be applied to political statements. For example, you can find out whether or not there are still "homeless" people on the streets, or how many people are covered or excluded from their country's health systems, or, another internationally famous example, although it concerns US domestic policy, George W. Bush in the 1988 presidential campaign said, or didn't say: "Read my lips. There will be no new taxes."[26]

Jamieson's concern lies in the dynamic between the press and politicians, a dynamic

---

26 Kathleen Jamieson (1992), *Dirty Politics*, Oxford, Oxford Press, 1992

that is dragging the public into what she and Joseph Cappella call a "spiral of cynicism". This self-destructive dynamic, they say, is being boosted by the fact that journalists increasingly believe that politicians' speeches are not substantive and that they analyze them according to a sieve of analysis related to the hidden agendas they imply, political leaders realize that the press reacts immediately to the kind of discourse in which conflict is valued over consensus, assertion over argument, strategy over content, producing their presentations accordingly in order to keep the spotlight on them.[27] In other words, each side argues that the cynical discourse about reality is what the other side is promoting and wants to present as the truth, with the consequent effects of skepticism and the emotional and intellectual distancing of the public from the different actors involved.

Researchers who study the behavior of the American public in relation to political leaders, their campaigns and government action, show that there is a real lack of commitment on the part of the public, both in relation to the press and in relation to the political process.[28] This disengagement can be minimized, according to Jamieson, if the candidates' proposals can be tested by each of the proponents and their opponents, by the press and by the public, if politicians know that we expect them to commit to defending the governance projects set out through argument, and if they responsibly agree to defend their proposals or those proposed to them by others.[29]

In *Dirty Politics,* K. Jamieson uses theories of argumentation to explain why the first test of a political statement is whether it is factually accurate.[30] In a deliberative discourse, argument should be its essential structure - understood both as the organizing process of disciplined thought, because it uses logical resources, and as signaling an interaction between two or more sets of related statements, one of which is necessarily a conclusion and the other statements are the premises that lead to that conclusion.

The author is under no illusions as to how the use of arguments is far from widespread in the proposals and speeches of American politicians, but she also knows that an assertion necessarily refers to facts that support it, unless it is made in a frivolous and irresponsible manner. Traditionally, argument was seen as a way of demonstrating the truth or validity of a proposition about something or other. It is along these lines that Jamieson believes it is possible to identify the existence of verifiable truths of fact in

---

27 Joseph Capella and Kathleen Jamieson (1997), *Spiral of Cynicism, The Press and the Public Good,* Oxford, Oxfor press, 1997:237.

28 Id. p,p:110-208.

29 Kathleen Jamieson (1992), *Dirty Politics,* p. 216.

30 Id., p. 217.

political discourse.[31]

With the aim of helping voters to form their own opinions in the time given to them to consider their choices, the time of the campaign, and the consequent decision made by casting their vote in the ballot box, these research groups try to convey the idea that even the facts studied in the statements that turn out to be opposed to the views of the world that structure the researcher's private life, will not be treated carelessly, as this is not sufficient cause for them to hide or mask them. They lend credibility to their analyses by evoking the factor of trust in the impartiality of the agents involved, because the events they analyze refer to facts that evoke the general interest of the population, which, they say, in all cases overrides the personal interests of the individual investigating them.

I believe that the validity of these investigations is attributed to the fact that they have publicly published their results and presented their methods of analysis, subject to verification by the academic community, but also by the press, among others. These fact-checking groups came about with the ambition of reinforcing the credibility of journalists' work using the rules of scientific work and what this brings in terms of believing in the credibility of the results with the reading community, and at the same time offering a framework for comparative judgements on the candidates' proposals in order to clarify for voters the differences that characterize each discourse.

In December 2003, the Annenberg Public Policy Research Center launched the project "The Annenberg Political Factcheck". This center is directed by philosopher Kathleen Jamieson and belongs to the Annenberg School for Communication at the University of Pennsylvania in the USA. This project with the general name of "factchck.org." presents itself to its target audience, American voters, with the aim of "reducing the level of disappointment and confusion with US politics", as you can read in its online presentation. It proposes to carry out this task by carefully researching the discursive interventions of the political subjects with the most prominent role in the American state and society. It should be noted that this group was created to react to a situation that we can classify as one of disinformation regarding political affairs.

One of the causes, in the opinion of the group of researchers, of voter disillusionment with political life is because they are confused by the presence of multiple communications with contradictory signals issued by politicians, which are not given specific critical treatment by journalists, who most of the time limit themselves to describing discursive events, recording communicational behaviour, without

---

31 Id. pp.203-236.

contextualizing them. This situation was identified as likely to contribute to an instrumental state of social communication, an issue that is insufficiently observed and resolved by the work of journalists in their classic media.

Under the financial and ethical auspices of the Annenberg Foundation[32] , the project of the American academy in Pennsylvania applies the general normative principles that guide the manifesto of the host institution, and it does so in an almost completely autonomous way in relation to the interest groups, profit or otherwise, of whoever holds political power. Principles which, in the declaration of the foundation's objectives, are announced as being interested in promoting a) the improvement of communication in order to contribute to the improvement of public welfare, and b) the development of means to make the sharing of ideas and knowledge more effective.[33]

Hannah Arendt realized that the most radical and lasting effect of a society exposed to constant disinformation is that, after a while, there is an absolute refusal on the part of citizens to believe in the truth of anything. It's not just the development of a skeptical feeling towards official sources of information, which would also have the immediate effect of making the propagated reality less effective[34] , but a generalization of this feeling towards the possibility of the existence of realities with different truth values.

If anything goes, nothing goes, then my emotional attachment needs no rational justification. The notion of the existence of a criterion for judging the value of truth is lost. This is a serious social problem, with a deeper dimension even *in* relation to the already serious case of taking lies for true reality, insofar as it affects one of the senses that guides the individual in their orientation in the real social world[35] : the sense necessary for their social survival, which implies that in the relationships they maintain with others, and between everyone and the reality that surrounds them, their ability to distinguish between what is true and what is false remains intact. And, as we know from studies in communication theory, the inability, or indifference, to distinguish between what is in fact true and what is a lie also affects one's personal relationship with oneself,

---

[32] Walter H. Annenberg (1908-2002), publisher, producer, diplomat and philanthropist, after founding the Annenberg School of Communication at the University of Pennsylvania in 1958 and the Annenberg School of Communication at the Univ. of Southern Calfornia in 1971, created the Annenberg Foundation. of Southern Calfornia in 1971, he created the Annenberg Foundation, with the purpose of serving for the research, development and application of ways that make the sharing of ideas and knowledge more effective, in a theoretical line that admits the promotion of public well-being through an improved communication process.

[33] Cf : http://www.whannenberg.org/

[34] A phenomenon that we know has happened, as David Beetham points out on page 107 of his aforementioned book, in countries where there has been, or is, a state attempt to totally control the news media, preventing the free circulation of ideas.

[35] Id., p.50.

so that the process of identity formation is jeopardized. Lies are no longer taken as a means to an end, hypothetically considered to be useful for oneself or one's group, but truth and lies are confused in such a way that the notion of differentiation is lost.

The American fact-checking service (Factchck.org)[36] has as its epigraph one of the most famous sayings of the late Democratic senator Daniel Patrick Moynihon, which goes like this: "Everyone is entitled to their own opinion, but not to their own fact".[37] It is under the conceptual framework defined by this maxim that the group works to identify the "political spin" that exists in political communication, i.e. it investigates the process that presents itself in its many communicative forms as an attempt to guarantee the most sought-after objective: that of winning more votes, even at the cost of the truth content of political messages.

It is true that without a theoretical contextualization, this maxim could reinforce the reaction of those who believe that there is a totalizing and coercive principle, and therefore a violent one, in all those who demand the presentation, always illusory but no less castrating, of the absolute fact as the maximum duty in the work of informing the public. If you understand, however, that the acceptability of a fact as true implies a communicational process of rational acceptance that involves the participation of members of a community with linguistic competence[38] , then you will understand that this maxim represents a goal in the work of investigation which, in practice, will have the aim of reconciling the voting public with the probability that the question of truth is present, and can be tested, in the statements made by candidates for election.[3839]

Moynihon's maxim presents itself to the working group as the description of an attitude and a method that the researchers will have to use with the care of someone who knows the subject of discussion, but without the inhibition of someone who is afraid to evoke factual accuracy in order to validate a discourse in terms of its degree of truth, fairness, comprehensibility and correctness.

The "factcheck" research began by checking the content of a paid advertisement that candidate Jonh Edwards broadcast on American television in September 2003 when he was campaigning for the position of Democratic presidential candidate, competing for

36 Cf. http://en.wikipedia.org/wiki/Daniel Patrick Moynihan

37 "Everyone is entitled to their opinion, but not their own fact."

38 In Apel, at the limit, an ideal community of speakers, which takes us to another dimension of discursive analysis, a transcendental level of investigation into the rules of language that allow us to define and distinguish the validity of what is said.

39 Members of a community are able to evaluate the coherence of the statement and the credibility of the speaker, even though this ability is common to the species and does not depend on any singular characteristic resulting from the personal will of each person.

the nomination to contest the November 2004 American presidential elections with George W. Bush (in Portugal this type of political advertising is illegal).[40] In this ad, J. Edwards addressed all viewers, claiming that the American state under the Bush administration would be protecting large corporations to the detriment of the rest of the taxpayers, who would see their taxes increase while the millionaires would make more and more profit and support their expansionist economic policies.

Three months later, the "factcheck" service began publishing its work online with an article asking whether or not it was a fact that Bush had, up to that point in his term in office, protected big business to the detriment of ordinary citizens. The article refutes and corrects the content of Edwards' statements, using statistical data and expert analysis.[41] This was the start of a page that was to have a remarkable success with journalists, politicians and, above all, civil society.

Since then, dealing not only with the material collected during the campaign which ended in November 2004 with the re-election of George Bush, but also with what government institutions have subsequently said in the exercise of their functions, the service has presented a series of articles every month dealing with the most diverse topics, as long as the researchers suspect that there is a disrespectful use of the facts, regardless of who the enunciator is or from which political quarter he comes.[42]

The national and international visibility of the site has led them to strengthen their team in order to meet the expectations of their readers, who trust them and turn to them as the ultimate guarantee of enlightenment. Their list of articles up to the time of writing, July 1, 2017, includes hundreds of research and analytical works. One of the latest, from April 29, 2017, analyzes the first hundred days of Donald Trump's presidency, exposing the recurring lies that the American president has made, and analyzing the fulfillment of electoral promises. On the website's homepage, you can access the videos with the analysis of the statements.

Watch the video "100 Days of President Trump's Whoppers - FactCheck.org" and see how the factcheck.org team analyzes the images, the words, and highlights what is less clear or false in the content of the president's statements, from his inauguration speech to the present day.[43] But it also reposes the truth about many of the rumors, many

---

[40] At the end of the campaign, the Democratic presidential candidate was John Kerry, with John Edwards nominated as the US vice-presidential candidate.

[41] Cf. http://www.factcheck.org/

[42] With the exception of December 2004, there were no entries.

[43] https://www.youtube.com/watch?v=38 LSHNvHUY (video The decline of American politics, and how to fix it | by Kathleen Hall Jamieson | TEDxMidAtlantic) Published 31/03/2017

of them equally false, that are made about the president's actions or decisions.

The 2016 elections between Hillary Clinton and Donald Trump turned the phenomenon of fake news, rumors and hearsay, which has always existed in the host of political confrontations in human history, into the main protagonist. Fake news was not just another means of combat in the political arena, it was used without hesitation as the main political weapon that contributed to disinformation and deliberate confusion among the electorate, rather than clarifying the issues that mattered to citizens. But above all, they were used as a weapon of character assassination. By whom? With what intentions at all? We are also investigating whether or not there was interference by state agencies or groups of connected individuals with the malicious intention of interfering in the electoral processes taking place around the world, particularly in the USA, the UK and France. Preliminary investigations point to the existence of websites originating in Russia, Macedonia, Romania and also in the US itself, which publish fraudulent news, sustained by the rapid proliferation of social media such as Facebook and Twitter, among others.

We know that deliberately confusing voters leaves them less able to make informed decisions, which is why the United Nations issued a joint statement on what they consider to be a serious threat to democracy around the world: fake news, disinformation and propaganda.[44] In this statement issued last March, the right to truth in information is defended as inviolable, but attention is also called for the fight against fake news to be carried out with respect for freedom of expression. It is feared that the reactions against fake news will also be directed against the taking of positions that do not please the powers that be.

The serious problem is that it becomes permissible to deny the facts in the name of discrediting reality, admitting that the criteria for distinguishing the true from the false are weak and relative.

Studies carried out by Sam Wineburg and Sarah McGrew at Stanford University show that 82% of pupils in the third cycle of studies (in Portugal this corresponds to pupils in the 7th to 9th grades) were unable to distinguish factual news from advertising. At the other higher education levels, secondary school and university, the numbers of those who accepted false statements as being true, not having the resources developed to

[44] On 3-3-2017, the United Nations published a declaration on: http://www.ohchr.org/ lavouts/15/WopiFrame.aspx?sourcedoc=/Documents/Issues/Expression/JointDeclaration3March2017.doc&action=default&DefaultItemOpen=1

evaluate the news, were also very high.[45]

How did communication academics go from announcing the successful digital campaign of presidential candidate Barack Obama in 2008[46] , to the current moment of suspicion regarding Donald Trump's use of the same media? What has changed is the content, not the media. They continued to allow the same proximity to the citizen, without intermediaries, as in the Obama campaigns. It's just that the lack of media, which is so convenient for any candidate who wants to build a direct bridge to their electorate, becomes a major problem when there are no scruples on the part of the candidates about using lies as a weapon/news, and readers or listeners are not prepared to do the fact-checking themselves and consequently reject this disinformation. The situation became so extreme that Facebook founder Mark Zuckerberg, who never wanted to take positions he considered political, was forced on December 15, 2016, to admit on his own Facebook page that as news distributors, his technology company was being used as a platform to disseminate and implement political discourse based on rumors and unverified news, so he had to take responsibility for defending the social space from the amount of false information that was circulating permissibly freely.

Feeling the pressure between keeping the channel open in the name of free expression and proceeding in such a way as to restrict the free, rapid and impactful circulation of unconfirmed statements, facebook technicians are proposing a set of tools to identify fraudulent news,[47] and have announced collaboration with fact-checking organizations such as factcheck. org and Politifact, among others.org" and "Politifact", but also with the fact-finding divisions of newspapers such as "The Washington Post" and "ABCNews", among others, allowing users to identify and denounce false or dubious news.

---

[45] https://sheg.stanford.edu/upload/V3LessonPlans/Executive%20Summarv%2011.21.16.pdfhttp://www.edweek.org/ew/articles/2016/11/02/whv-students-cant-google-their-wav-to.html

[46] One article among hundreds published then:

https://stratecherv.com/2016/fake-news/ ("Fake news" by Ben Thompson)
- "No internet, no Obama" by political scientist Michael Cornfiled, presented and explored in:
http://www.scielo.br/scielo.php?script=sci arttext&pid=S0104-44782009000300004
Book bringing together articles by researchers on Obama's use of social media:
https://books.google.pt/books?id=Sa2-AAAAQBAJ&pg=PA8&lpg=PA8&dq=michael+cornfield+no+internet+no+obama&source=bl&ots=JiDcccPAMs&sig=EeLq6yMJEo9LElB3w-Vh3 t6Vg8&hl=en-EN&sa=X&ved=0ahUKEwj 6rwE9OfUAhUEWxoKHUjiC5YQ6AEIW zAP#v=onepage&q=michael%20cornfield%20no%20internet%20no%20obama&f=false

[47] http://www.niemanlab.org/2016/12/clamping-down-on-viral-fake-news-facebook-partners-with-sites-like-snopes-and-adds-new-user-reporting/

American researchers have been experimenting with solutions to this now global problem, ranging from the proposal to intensify media education for all young students, in order to teach them to behave as fact-checkers themselves, preparing them to analyze sources and critically question the content of the news,[48] including those like Emily Willingham[49] who propose that teaching media analysis should be done by applying the steps of the scientific method to news analysis (observe, question, hypothesize, test and analyze information, conclude and act), or Filippo Menczen who developed the digital tool "Hoaxy"[50] through which we try to identify news without evidence or with little evidence to support the alleged facts. These researchers talk about the existence of an industry producing fake news, many of which originate from "bots" to get people to click on a particular website to disseminate information in a biased and one-sided way, or to be suggested news and information that their digital profile has defined as being more to their liking, preventing them from being confronted with ideas opposed to their own, placing them in a kind of ideological bubble, living in a world that feeds itself without contradiction.

The existence of individuals who design algorithms according to analytical parameters biased by prejudice or discrimination makes us lose confidence in the neutrality of mathematical programs. And these are at the basis of many of the decisions that institutions make about us, the granting of credit by a bank, for example.

The trend at the beginning of 2017 has been for big tech companies, particularly search engines like Google, to help users identify and flag pages containing fake news. The way seems to be to give users more knowledge to do their own checks and develop their skepticism about what they read, see or hear.

In 2017, politicians also tend to label as fake news those that come from groups or individuals opposed to their own ideas, creating a maelstrom that confuses the truth and the falsity of reality. More radical supporters of US President D. Trump have even branded some of the most influential media outlets, which are more critical of the political leader's policies and behavior, as producers of "fake news". If the finger is pointed in all directions, what is the line of demarcation? Where do we find the criteria that allow us not only to distinguish truth from falsehood, but also for people to

[48] "You're the fact checker now", by Sam wineburg and Sarah McGrew https ://medium.com/stanford-alumni/youre-the -fact-checker-now-60103eaeaf3 a

[49] https://www.forbes.com/sites/emilywillingham/2016/11/28/a-scientific-approach-to-distinguishing- real-from-fake-news/#2dda53e82bd8

[50] https://hoaxy.iuni.iu.edu/faq.html

recognize its reliability, objectivity and impartiality? How can we believe in something again? If uncomfortable facts are omitted or dressed up as inventions, where can you go back or forward to get an objective point of view?

When Arendt wrote her texts, the manipulation of behavior by discourse, the invention of rumors and the defense of lies had also been a communicational practice of the German totalitarian regime from which she had fled, and in the Western world the media and political actors have always had their own agendas and prejudices, no qualms about using lies to their advantage, and there were even deep academic concerns about the effects of the media's "agenda setting" on the formation of public opinion. But in 2017, this concern was exacerbated by what, as K. Jamieson said in his TED TALK presentation, "The decline of American politics and how to fix it", we don't want to see become a "new normal".

On October 28, 2005, factcheck's concerns consisted, for example, of analyzing advertising on California TV channels paid for by the pharmaceutical industry. On the site we have access to the videos with the selected ads and, after a summary, an analysis of their content. Be careful with the sources they select to present their information, they always use data from independent associations. This is how they start by presenting data on the amount spent by the industry on advertising in defense of their "proposition78", which then referred to a prescription program defended by the pharmaceutical companies, against the amount spent by the proponents of a measure (proposition 79) which aimed at a discount program negotiated by the companies to cover a greater number of middle-class patients. This group is mainly made up of trade unions and consumer associations.

What interests us is the way the "factcheck.org." team analyzes the images, the words, and highlights what is unclear or false in the content of the ads, always ending with a bibliography on the topic addressed. They do not take a position on the rightness or wrongness of the measure proposed by each of the proponents, they analyze the content of the statements, make comparative studies with other programs already in place in other states and present statistics. It will be the readers who will make their decision and value the messages presented to them with their choice. It's clear that there is an appreciation of the facts in that the team has chosen these advertisements to process and not any other, but from the moment the selection is made, the type of appreciation assumed is that of the information and the verification of the statements.

Speaking to the newspaper "Penn Current",[51] , the director of "Factcheck.org", journalist Brooks Jackson said that this project came about during the run-up to the 2004 presidential campaign, because he had never realized in his life as a political journalist that there would be an election race as long as this one, and that therefore its monitoring by communication specialists was essential in order to understand whether so much exposure to political debates would make people more aware of the manipulative strategies used to create political facts through "Spin" techniques, or whether, on the contrary, these "marketing" techniques would have a better chance of succeeding in their attempts to shape behavior.

In the survey studies conducted by the National Annenberg Election Survey, it was concluded that both things happened. Even voters who said they didn't learn anything from paid political ads ended up absorbing information and believing what they were told. There is also a proliferation of 527 associations, which are organizations made up of influential individuals, mostly liberal professionals, who are using attack ads to influence or try to influence nominations and elections.[52] On the other hand, there is the chance of having more time to unmask the "spin" techniques used in these ads, such as using quotes out of context, selectively using knowledge of facts, making statements assuming certain facts to be true when they have yet to be proven, among others. [53]

On November 2, 2004, the service told its readers that it would continue its work even after the elections. At that time, it underwent its first reformulation (it would no longer analyze the speeches of political leaders in the campaign) and would now monitor government speeches, state speeches and, as we have recently read, the speeches of other institutions of power, such as the large economic groups.[54] The team feels the need for external validation, which is why on November 23, 2004 it presented the results of a survey of its subscribers, reporting that the vast majority of subscribers who answered the survey considered its articles to be accessible and reliable.[55]

---

51 Cf. http://www.upenn.edu/pennnews/current/2004/092304/research.html

52 Cf. http://www.gnossos.com/webhelp/What_is_a_527_Organization_.htm

53 "Spin" was the acronym for the term originally used by PR people to mean "Significant Progress In the News".

54 " If history is any guide, there will be plenty of distortions and falsehoods to expose even in a non - election year, and we intend to monitor and report on the major factual claims being made from Washington through the remainder of 2004, and into 2005 and beyond. Watch the "announcements" section on the home page for updates", at http://www.factcheck.org/article299.html.

55 "More than 21,000 FactCheck.org subscribers responded to our online survey conducted Nov. 13-19. That's roughly 30% of all those who signed up to get our articles emailed to them. Overwhelmingly, those who responded found our articles clear and easy to understand, politically unbiased, reliable, and helpful in forming opinions about the candidates and their positions. Journalists make up only 2 percent of respondents, but most of them found our articles helpful and nearly half quoted us as an authority.

Take a look at the article of September 16, 2005, which for me sums up the excellence of the work of the American fact-checking team. In an investigation that they claim took months, we are given a chronology of events/speeches/actions related to the devastation of Hurricane Katrina. A chronology that begins months before (more precisely thirteen months before, on July 23rd, with the announcement by the Federal Emergency Management Agency (FEMA)) the natural phenomenon hit the state of Louisiana hard as a grade 4 storm. The reading we are allowed to make of the most important things that happened or were said by political leaders during this period gives us a clear idea of what a "fact-checking" job is: presenting the statements/events that are significant for understanding what the political power did (and there is never an evaluation of what the political power should have done). That analysis, or commentary, is left to the reader). The article is based on a set of sources that are truly remarkable in their breadth, and which support its information.

In 2017, the "Factcheck.org" website has a video entry[56] and a paper entry on how to stop the spread and importance of fake news. And the entries on fact-checking what is said about the American President are constant.

In England, Channel 4[57] developed a website where it presented a project similar to the American factcheck, claiming that it was doing its job as a public service: the aim was to encourage its readers to debate public issues and take a greater interest in political topics. However, since this group, unlike the American team, was made up entirely of journalists, the intention of this project was to enhance digital journalism for the first time. This objective was absent from the more academic concerns of the Americans. However, the creators of the English site call it a replica of the American correspondent site, which, like its counterpart, began its activity with the publication of an online article during an election campaign. In March 2005, Channel 4's "factcheck" began monitoring the UK general election campaign and concluded its work with the publication of the last article of this first period of work on the day after the election, May 6th.[58]

Jon Bernstein, the editor-in-chief of the English site, justifies his work in contrast to that of journalists working in the traditional press: "Because of their peculiarity, newspapers often carry a certain amount of critical baggage, and consumers often have

---

Teachers made up 10 percent of the respondents, and one in three used our articles in class.One in six who responded worked in the 2004 presidential campaign at some level. Few Kerry nor Bush workers thought our articles made their opponent more careful about stating the facts, however", in http://www.factcheck.org/article300.html.

[56] https://www.youtube.com/watch?v=AkwWcHekMdo

[57] Cf. http://www.channel4.com/news/factcheck/

[58] Cf. http://www.channel4.com/news/factcheck/quote.isp7idM69

preconceived notions about the origin of that publication."[59] It is therefore understood that the nature of the medium in which the articles are published, and the clear presentation of the objectives and mission with which the identified team presents itself, will make a difference in the fight for credibility in what is advertised.[60]

By giving the reader access to the articles analyzed, but already divided into major themes (crime, economics, education, health, immigration and asylum, and others) and presenting a forum for discussion, the English "factcheck" differs from the American methodology. However, I think that the message conveyed to us by the frame that makes up the English "page" gives us a less rigorous image than the one conveyed by the American service. First of all, the existence of a forum implies the existence of a free and public space for readers to intervene, which is generally characterized by an excess of unsubstantiated opinions. Which, let's face it, in a "site" that wants to be the paradigm of a type of treatment of discourses through tests of the truth of their content, could appear as a strange and paradoxical element, since the intention is to highlight a work that wants to stand out from the multiplicity of opinions that are spread. Not that facts can't be discussed, but we have to assume that at some point the discussion will have to reach a conclusion, and if that conclusion isn't reached by the experts who tested it, who will reach it?

Something else I think also contributes to maintaining a misleading image of the British project. The fact that Channel 4 presents its "factcheck" service as a service whose motto is "keeping politicians honest", which, as we can compare, is the appropriation of a power that the American service does not assume, because it implies that it is the responsibility of voters to keep politicians honest. Factcheck doesn't run for election, it's a political speech analysis service, independent of the parties (it doesn't run for or against any party, but it's not a political party either).

The academic "site" of the American service does not incur in this kind of conflict because it understands that its imposition on power is based on a generalized information base of voters. Let me say that this is because they are better grounded theoretically by the presence of K. Jamieson in their analysis group. You're not running against power, you're running to clarify the communicative actions of that power.

[59] "The nature of newspapers means that they often have a certain amount of critical baggage, and consumers often have a preconceived notion of where that publication is coming from,"

Cf. http://www.channel4.com/news/factcheck/

[60] FactCheck.org as a "consumer advocate for voters".

In Portugal, civil society has so far not created a monitoring service of a similar nature to the American projects. But the public media have already started their own fact-checking model, whether in print, on television or online. They do this intermittently, and usually during election campaigns, but the dogital newspaper "Observador", for example, has a "fact check" service that it has been publishing with some regularity since June 2015. It is mainly through public administration bodies that electoral acts are monitored and disciplined. This role, the disciplinary one, involves the intervention of a body that monitors and guarantees that the democratic rules are respected in elections, submitting problems relating to electoral litigation to the courts, which will judge whether or not the constitutional rules have been complied with.

Since their appearance until today, fact-checking services have changed the way they present themselves in political and communicational society. At the time, they had a disciplinary function, but this was born out of the very public exposure of their content to a large number of public opinion-makers who reacted to them, these services did not monitor or enforce compliance with rules, nor were they directly committed to defending and promoting human rights, because "spin politics" does not directly challenge, for example, the right to freedom of expression. These services allowed us to see the concern that certain groups of citizens, whether or not they were media professionals, had about clarifying what in public discourse could contribute to the mystification of political action or the clarification of what political work and political campaigns are in a democracy. This is different from the kind of evocation of any concrete power of control that, in Portugal, is assumed by the Courts.

Nowadays, fact-checking services have taken on a more assertive role in defending and restoring the truth in political discourse and we feel that the tone, the list of rules and advice for citizens to defend themselves against the social effects of the spread of fake news, and the scrutiny of political speeches, is more that of political activists defending democracy, the space for public deliberation, and fair rules in communication, by urging that we all take care to confirm the facts presented. But if the service made its debut in 2005, that didn't stop the election at the end of 2016 of a political leader who has a very elusive notion of truth and the "gravitas" of office.

These services are at the service of voters and citizens, but they do not induce them to want to know, to want to vote, to deliberate rationally. If a large group of citizens are angry and frustrated with their class of political leaders, rational means of control and scrutiny of political speeches are indifferent to them, almost obstacles to them continuing on a path they want completely different from the one proposed by the usual politicians. At that point, a politician who uses the social media in a loud way and then draws the attention of the traditional media, has a perfect megaphone for the crowd, and if he manages to say what those ears want to hear at that moment, how can he tell them to distinguish between truth and lies? So that they don't go along emotionally, but reserve their adherence until they have proof of trust in the person's character and actions? Do we know why these people made this choice? Or why most of the others didn't even bother to go and vote?

Do we know how, since the 1980s, religious and political propagandists have been extremizing their messages without democratic reactions being unequivocal signs that they would not allow themselves to be overtaken by certain discursive standards? Do people have reasons for doing what they do? Are those reasons publicly debatable and can they justify their decisions? If so, they have not been manipulated. We may not like these reasons or we may arrogantly underestimate them, but they are rational, they should be understood and they can be explained. Now, what if communication strategies have acted on their capacity for discernment, affecting it and distorting their conception of reality, distracting them from the essential and focusing them on the superfluous? Instead of discussing the failures of my government and national health program, I can, as Trump has done, distract the public in general and the media in particular with misogynistic messages on Twitter, attacking political talk show hosts who don't agree with me, or raising the tone of bitterness towards any rival country that might stoke the patriotic feelings of my fellow citizens. Attention is diverted from the essential.

Let's not underestimate this communication strategy or the citizens who are attracted to it. Because either we are in fact facing a strategy of social control and behavioral reorientation in line with more radical ideological visions, and this should set all minds racing to find solutions for the defense of democracy, or we are facing yet another episode, brief and fleeting like all other events in history when contextualized on the scale of universal time, of the exercise of power for power's sake, until power - some political epiphenomenon. Just as we must be able to foresee the social consequences of this kind of exercise of power, we must be vigilant.

In Portugal, we should also carry out a rigorous survey of the number of times that opinion articles or interventions by journalists on radio or television programs have defended the idea that no politician speaks, or can speak, the truth in a political campaign. It would be interesting to know what stage our spiral of cynicism has reached.

The chain of sequences linking ethics and politics did not begin when ethics became autonomous from the fields of moral law and religious reasoning, but it was with the emergence of rational ethics, or ethics based on *logos*, that they became paradoxically related realities. Ordinary men, evoking the authority of rational analysis, began to criticize their city's ways of life and government, proposing models for guiding individual and collective conduct based on previously unknown criteria and working methods that did not depend entirely on the convenience of the powerful of the moment or on divine instructions. It happened from the moment that critical thinking began, in other words, when philosophy appeared.

Beginning with considerations based on an awareness of and reflection on the ultimate meaning and purpose of human action, this was a time of discovering the human condition in the world and reflecting on the natural and historical conditions that gave rise to it, but also on those that could be transformed through the production of norms that were intended to be universal and above sociocultural circumstances, in order to improve the character of each individual or life in common.

Hannah Arendt identifies this "midpoint in the spiritual process" as an axis in universal history that runs through the 5th century B.C. A period in our history in which, as she writes, all the basic principles of our beliefs were created[61] . It was the time when the existence of a secular normative influence was admitted for the first time, based on the reflections of the wise on the orientations of actions that went beyond the mere description of natural laws, traditional social rules, or the dictates supported by magical-religious explanations that regulate societies. It was a time to observe and study human behavior, and to try to link the formation of individual character to its effect on public life. Well, it didn't happen all at once and by a circumscribed group, but it did happen in a certain spatially and socially circumscribed society and at a defined time.[62]

Prodicus of Ceos testified to this original and controversial link between ethics and politics, claiming that there was a visible link between these two different ways of acting in the world, philosophical and political ethics, and that this mediating figure was represented by the sophists[63] . According to Prodicus, the sophist would be the figure who would then be able to unite the role of the philosopher (who thinks about the city)

[61] Hannah Arendt, *Men in Dark Times,* p.107
[62] Werner Jaeger, *Paideia*, Editoriasl Aster, Lisbon, 1979, pp. 311-357.
[63] Maria Helena Rocha Pereira; Helade, Coimbra, 1982, p.259.

and that of the politician[64] (who governs the city), between the producer of universal principles and the author of political *praxis*.[65] This is an assertion that the philosopher Plato wanted to dispel by proclaiming the need for a philosopher who was himself the ruler of the city, thus eliminating the need for any mediating figure.

Ethics is an area of critical investigation in relation to existing conventional value systems, but not only that, it itself becomes a producer of moral concepts, which it seeks to substantiate and legitimize in the light of the universality defined by the human rational faculty. It becomes an area of philosophy that proposes a set of principles of action that indicate how individuals should behave. Ethics arose as a continuation of the efforts of wise men who sought to identify and legitimize what they understood to be general precepts of good practice or rules of a just and wise life, by reflecting on the powers and limits of human thought.

In the *Odyssey*, certain aspects of character are valued over others. The courage shown in battle is a highly prized value, along with the duty of hospitality, fear of the gods and obedience to the law, which together define the characteristics of a good government in any land. See for example the laudatory description by third parties of PeiK'lope's governmental action in the absence of her husband Ulysses .[66]

In another text, which also predates the systematized production of critical thought, we have a set of practical tips proposed by Hesiod in his text *Works and Days.* In this text, the author tries to appeal to good behavior through positive practical consequences (earthly glory for himself and his followers, by winning divine favor, or the possibility of achieving immortality). However, these principles regulating action, although they demonstrate the existence of concerns about the formation of character, do not have the dimension of the reflection inaugurated by Socrates and some of the Sophists, who gave human beings the autonomy to examine and describe themselves, because they were capable of producing rational knowledge about action and the rules of behavior in the city (from the citizen to the citizen - man, free and natural of Greece). There is a development and preparation of the government no longer according to the model of passing on knowledge from the aristocrat to his descendants, based exclusively on

[64] Carmen Soares, translator of Plato's *The Politician*, says that of the testimonies written and known to date, it is in this work by Plato that the term "politikos" is used for the first time. This noun was applied to a person who was involved in the government of the city. The author indicates that the current terms used to designate these individuals were "rhetores" (orators) or "strategoi" (generals), depending on the case.

[65] "[Sophists] are intermediaries between philosophers and politicians." (frg. 6 Diels), in Maria Helena Rocha Pereira,

[66] Odyssey, XIX, 107-114.

tradition and mythical narratives, but as a citizen in possession of his rational faculties and making use of his freedom of thought.

The new conceptions about man's place in the cosmos and in his community, as well as the speculations about the origin, nature and purpose of his actions, will have repercussions on ethics and politics. This is also where the fragility of the proposed philosophical ethical models lies, in relation to the confrontation with their own demand for legitimacy, which is intended to be universal, because if we analyze their proposals over a long period of time, we come across a multiplicity of definitions of what is meant by a good, just or virtuous action, and the identification of the supreme good.

This question, while pertinent and central, does not affect the other one, that of the link between politics and politics. This activity is limited to a period of time (that of legitimizing the exercise of the agent's power), and therefore to specific spatio-temporal circumstances, while ethics seeks to dominate chance, searching for universal principles that are not subject to variation and corruption over time and are rationally justifiable as regulators of private and public action.

The question of the beginning of this new intellectual attitude is also not without debate, as is the process of the primacy of one over the other. When sophists like Protagoras and philosophers like Socrates began their reflections on the nature and purpose of human action, regardless of the answers they had found up to that point, and followed a model of questioning similar to what naturalist philosophers had done when they wondered about the origin and nature of the cosmos, democracy had already been established as a form of government in Athens.

It wasn't for this reason that the philosophers emerged as theoretical defenders of this form of government in particular, because they realized right away how even the best form of government known until then could become corrupted and, in its decadent phase, serve the citizens just as badly as other more unjust and hated forms of government. In contrast, for example, to the Sophists, who coexisted openly with corrupted forms of democracy, appropriating their values and developing the pedagogical techniques necessary for any individual who then aimed to integrate and conquer the city's seats of power.

The condition of the very act of philosophizing, as it was conceived, meant that philosophers had to restrain themselves from trying to get involved in public affairs that resulted in the solution of practical issues, in order to free their analyses from constraints that were extrinsic to the method of investigating the truth; suspicion of the rhetorical techniques associated with winning over the opinion of the majority; disbelief at the traditional models of understanding behavior and guiding it, and a conception of pedagogy based on goals conditioned to the interests of each moment and each group. Even Plato, at the beginning of his intellectual journey, advocated a government of aristocrats of spirit as the most favorable counterpoint to a government of mass popular participation. A whole new intelligibility of the world is being born, with the creation of new concepts and new attitudes towards common life.

It seems then that philosophical ethics was born with the condition of trying to stay away from concrete political action, because both could cancel each other out in the struggle for dominance of one of the legitimization models proposed for regulating behavior. We don't think this was the case. And this is certainly due to the Sophists' connection to practical life, and, in turn, their connection to philosophy, through the latter's criticism of the latter's actions and pedagogical influence, and their concern with the common object of study.

They were also influenced by the action (and theories) that stemmed from their philosophical attitude, which, however paradoxical it may seem, never ceased to amaze their fellow citizens, captivating them with this new way of understanding and discussing the city's public affairs and bringing them to a more specialized and argumentative level of discussion. Proof of this is that the philosophers were listened to by many of the young people from wealthy families who would later hold public office, by those in positions of power in the city, by all the citizens who were available to discuss public affairs.

Philosophical schools and academies were highly frequented and academically regarded places. Before opening his Lyceum in Athens, Aristotle was asked to educate Alexander, son of King Philip II of Macedonia, the future Alexander the Great. The philosopher's pedagogy was making its way. However, philosophers were still subject to the legal and moral limits imposed by their city on all its citizens, and however unjust these laws might seem to them, they were just as bound to obey them as any of their fellow citizens.

It is a fact that many of the philosophers up to the 19th century often claimed to be far removed from the immediate and practical interests of many of their fellow citizens. This is a rhetorical defense mechanism against the domination of other ways of understanding the world which, by subjecting the will and being able to use coercive and legitimate law and order in this subjection, could curtail freedom or even physically eliminate the producer of any controversial alternative systems. Socrates is the first to say it: "Whoever is really committed to fighting for justice and wants to keep his life for a while, must necessarily keep himself a simple private individual, he cannot occupy himself with public affairs."[67]

Not being able to deal with public affairs as they are doesn't mean that you can't think of the best way for them to be carried out, with an ideal value in mind.

Since the beginning of the production of ethical-philosophical thought, we have had a confrontation between different proposals on the *modus operandis* of exercising power, with the one that actually assumed it in the city seeking to maintain its dominance by unbalancing the civil forces in its favor. And ethical philosophy never really dominated, except in the arguments exchanged between a master and his disciples, in manuals, and in the brief form of an outline, when there was an effective attempt to condition figures of power to the theoretical models proposed, as was the case with Plato in Syracuse[68] . However, their influence is claimed to be absolute over the government of each citizen's soul. Socrates will shift the importance of the display of public action to the pursuit of excellence in private action, and refocus energies on knowledge rather than its application in politics.

Ethical norms, relying on the force of conscience to impose themselves, only demonstrate their ability to influence behavior, while other norms, of a legal nature, are reinforced by institutions that can impose them externally and compulsorily. Legal norms present what a society in general is willing to accept as being the best for it in particular, in the name of custom or tradition, but also through the force of discussion and decision-making in assembly.

By producing laws, and ensuring that they are applied in an isonomic way (the law must be the same for everyone), the aim was to regulate behavior between individuals with interests as distinct from each other as those that make up a community. People accept the external coercive power associated with them, and the acceptance of its superimposition on any ethical theory, in the name of the known and established order.

---

[67] Plato, *Apology of Socrates,* 31 d

[68] Plato recounts three episodes as a councilor of state in the city of Syracuse, Sicily. In practice, he fulfilled what in theory was the philosopher's mission: not to shy away from helping to establish just political power when invited to do so. But with none of the city's governors did he succeed. His model of submitting power to knowledge and his proposals for laws were not accepted, and the philosopher who had thought to instruct the tyrant was instructed by him in the reality of political power that uses every means to sustain itself in office. Read a good summary in: Barros, Gilda Naecia Maciel, (2006) *Platao em Siracusa a Conversao do Tirano.* Consulted in September 2012.

It is no less true that the interest in theoretical reflection and rationalist pedagogy conditioned pedagogical and governing practices, if only through the systematic comparison of proposals with each other and the integration of certain proposed ethical norms into the political systems or behaviors in force. If this were not the case, if there were no influences whatsoever, the assembly of the people, albeit in the guise of a democratic decision, as Plato would say, would have been indifferent to Socratic pedagogy and would not have needed to bother with a trial and the awarding of capital punishment to a philosopher. Nor, over the centuries, would we have seen a strong conditioning of the dissemination of ethical-philosophical theories that were more dissonant with the established model of action, or seen the organization of strong police systems to monitor and punish dissident thoughts.

In classical antiquity, since ethics was initially geared towards proposing the most virtuous formation of individual character, and politics was a practical exercise in regulating public actions, a link was established between the two, firstly through the former's proposal of new and ideal models for the formation of individuals into potential rulers of the *polity*, but also through its criticism and social pressure on governing actions on the part of the intellectual elite.

They will tell us that from the nascent moment of this reflection on politics until its maturation, in the later works of Plato and Aristotle, there was a transformation of theory, in the sense of approaching practice, taking it not only as the object of reflection, as it had already been doing by systematizing models, but proposing possible improvements to legislative and executive action, which did not involve rejecting the state of affairs as it existed.

In fact, only Plato, and only in one of his most quoted works, *The Republic,* confronts the real model of city governance, implying a total renunciation of it, and gives as an alternative a model based on philosophical knowledge and practice. All the other philosophers, and even Plato in his later political works, such as *The Politician* and, above all, in the *Laws,* although critical of the forms chosen for governing the city, did so with the aim of organizing actions, classifying and systematizing them in the light of rational criteria of valuation. Criteria for exercising government according to the principles of justice, and making proposals for change and improvement. This required reflective consideration of all aspects of a public issue, to be conducted by men of understanding - those who are concerned with developing what is rational in themselves, according to truth and virtue.

The question arises: was it politics that had to give birth to ethics out of the need for the state to be provided with educated men to reflect on the creation and valuation of actions to provide for the government of the city, or was it ethics that consummated an intellectual and spiritual development that culminated, albeit indirectly, in influencing the processes of governance?

Werner Jaeger (1936) answers the two previous questions in the affirmative. For the author, the fourth century saw the creation of Pericles' state, which aimed to balance spirit and force. This provided sufficient freedom of thought for the production of new systems of understanding society and the individual, but these quickly emancipated themselves from external constraints and took on a *body of theory* with an autonomous and unique character in the history of culture.[69]

When, in the 4th century BC, the city of Athens tried to recover from the deep crisis in which it had been plunged, trying to recover from its material losses and its strategic failures in government and politics, it was in its ethical philosophy and in the proposals for models linked to the creation of ideals of state that the philosophical spirit and the forms of culture that resulted from it became manifest, which is what its heritage consists of.

What we will see in classical antiquity is an effort on the part of the philosophers to overcome this attempt to mediate between philosophy and politics, a position required by the sophists. Seeking to assume the role of educators or prescribers of action, the philosophers aimed to ensure that the principles produced by rational knowledge would shape practice, without devaluing the actions of intermediaries, through example and the learning of a new research method.

The criticism that was leveled at the time is similar to contemporary criticism, and encompasses all those thinkers who argue that there is a unity between ethics and politics, because, among other secondary reasons, it is argued that philosophy has relied on the matrix proposed by Socratic ethical thought, namely: ethics proposed as knowledge that would lead to a virtuous existence, or, in other words, the defense of universal principles of action at the cost of disregarding the effect of particular actions on them. It is commonly understood as a superimposition of the ideal over the real, or at least of a defense of perennial values over a historicist conception of them.

For many contemporary authors, particularly in the area of positivist law, who call it the "ethical imagination", this attempt to reflect on values, which is the production of

[69] Werner Jaeger, *Paideia*, Universidade Nova, 1979, pp. 447 to 456.

ethics, is nothing more than another narrative that adds nothing to the interpretation of human actions in terms of decision-making, or in terms of indicating concrete courses of action in each practical situation. Simon Blackburn reinforces this idea, as he believes that for all the practical dilemmas of our existence there is no theory that can serve as an absolute guide.

Aristotle was very clear in explicitly affirming the value of ethics for the political sphere and vice versa, establishing a strong relationship between the sphere that reflexively guides individual conduct and the other that deals with the best forms of practical life. Aristotle states that all philosophical contemplation, which involves searching for the truth about things, is manifested in everyday action.[70]

Human beings can only become ethical if they act. The inner life, research into the best ways of living, is not enough to produce the Aristotelian ethical man. Thinking about the purpose, and the best hypotheses for making it possible, is not enough to characterize ethics; we have to think about how to realize these theoretical presuppositions in action and act accordingly.

In the very first chapter of the *Nicomachean Ethics,* Aristotle speaks of politics as the activity that is best able to project daily life from fundamental principles. This Aristotelian position is the one to which all the intellectuals who defend the existence of a close relationship between the ethical dimension and politics have subordinated themselves to this day. Aristotle tells us that politics not only determines which sciences are necessary for the state and which each citizen should learn (strategy, economics and rhetoric, for example), but also legislates about the things that should be done and 71 those that should be avoided.

Where does this legislative capacity come from? From what can it design the means to achieve the goods most desired by all men? For Aristotle, these goods are unified in the most extreme of them, happiness *(eudaimonia).* Happiness is the supreme good that most men (and the most sophisticated, he adds) aim to achieve. And how can politics help them? If it starts from the application of fundamental principles, the author concludes. As Aristotle warns of the margin of error that opens up with the possibility of taking the means for the ends, and the mistakes that can be made when determining what happiness is supposed to be, philosophical research must be used to obtain such precision in the identification and definition of the good itself.

For Aristotle, happiness, since it seems to be a self-sufficient good of complete

[70] Aristotle, *The Nicomachean Ethics,* Lisbon, ed. Quetzal

fulfillment, will become the ultimate end of actions. It is now up to politics to create the material and historical conditions necessary for the realization of this good. The general interest is seen as more beautiful and divine than individual interest. And the activity of politics is to manage all the conflicting interests and make citizens excellent and capable of admirable actions.[71][72] According to what? According to "actions performed in accordance with ethical excellence", because these are what lead to happiness. Why? Because they are stable throughout life, because they give solidity in the midst of the contingencies to which we are subjected in daily life.

Happiness as a possibility or goal for individual and collective life, however, only has value if it can be practiced, lived. Actions performed in accordance with the idea of excellence bring about the good of that excellence, Aristotle tells us. As mere possibilities, without becoming active in order to be realized as actions, excellent goods are nothing more than activities of the soul. Politics serves this purpose: to actualize, to work on and to bring the supreme good to its extremes, because the politician, as an expert in creating a better citizenship, must know about the activities of the soul.[73]

For the first philosophers who debated this issue, politics had to reflect on the ways of updating the best government for the promotion and defense of just principles of action (Socrates and Plato) or happy actions.

For most other men, politics was understood as a means of attaining positions of power and then, once these had been attained, seeking to ensure legitimacy for the best use of the means at the service of that government in guiding behavior and making decisions, according to their own designs (autocracy) or those of the majority of citizens (democracy), but always taking into account the interests and practices of the individuals in the society in question.

The behavior of the philosophers who theorized about the best forms of government, concentrated on self-examination and on appreciating the actions of others, by not allowing themselves to be taken in by the greed for political consecration, deserved admiration from their fellow citizens, but also repudiation.

The more the philosophers developed a critical attitude towards the social and cultural contingencies of action and an almost total indifference to the honors associated with positions of power, the more unsettling their action became. The attraction they exerted on their citizens was not quantitatively greater than the retraction of their

71 Idem, 1094b1
72 Idem, 1099b30
73 Idem ,1102a20

influence and the strangeness of their life choices. Proof of this were the thirty or so citizens who, being able to make the difference in the final count, out of the five hundred or so who judged the philosopher Socrates, decided to add their vote to those who were against the cause of the sage.

If we read the book *The Apology of Socrates, we* will see how the discomfort felt by many citizens towards the figure of the philosopher consists precisely in their incomprehension of the behavior of someone who acts in the public sphere, advising each citizen on the best way to lead their life, dealing in his research with all the issues related to the government of the city, but who refuses to deal with public affairs in public office.

The decision of the popular assembly, in the case of Socrates, will reinforce the philosopher's attitude of defense, deepening his aim of withdrawing from social life, calling for concentration on the inner life, reinforcing his character as a critical observer and proposer of better ways to update active participation in the public sphere, sacrificing any will of his to act or participate. Plato will still try to counteract this fate, thinking of historically creating the idealized government of philosophers, but he will not succeed in his practice, as his relationship with the tyrants of Syracuse reminds us, who did not allow themselves to be educated by the philosopher, nor did they reform their political regime. However, their intention to use Plato for personal promotion had an effect. Twenty-four centuries later, why are they talked about? Because three times the philosopher thought he could educate them to become philosopher-kings. He failed, but in that failure he brought the Dionysos into the history of thought; associated with the philosopher, they didn't collect wisdom, but projected themselves into posterity.

In classical antiquity, philosophers didn't want to teach how to live better in a state as it was, they wanted to teach how to live in a state as it should be. Philosophers did not aspire to the role of sophists, self-proclaimed teachers of virtue, to guide the behavior of their disciples in the social and political contexts in which they were integrated.

For Socrates, who shared his time in history with a great statesman like Pdricles, the state had to submit to the only possible norm, the matrix of all others: knowledge of the truth. Only this standard could lead to action guided by the idea of justice. The philosopher argued that powerful men, those who govern public life, are mostly evil and perverse, because for him the practice of unjust and impious actions is necessarily associated with the facilities granted by power as it is experienced.[74]

---

[74] Plato, *Gorgias,* 525e and 526ª , Ed, 70, 1992, pp.211

The philosopher is advised to distance himself from public life and seek only the truth, without regard for the honors that please the majority, because his detachment will be rewarded, if not in this time of the body, in the time and dimension of the spirit. But in an eminently political society, whose citizens' participation in assemblies was the alpha and omega of public existence, the attitude of distancing oneself from these stages of action marked a position that was also political; disregard for the methods used to take care of public affairs was, in itself, a political choice.

Socrates would suffer the consequences of this way of life at his trial and public condemnation. However, he persisted until his death in exhorting that the exclusive use of political rhetoric should be at the service of the good and justice. But what is the good? It is the value from which all others derive and which will serve as a model for all action, Plato tells us. And he puts it into Socrates' mouth, when he describes the days of captivity of his sentenced master, that the good, the beautiful and the just *are* one and the same thing, and that this was the *arete,* the virtue, that every man should achieve.[75]

Why use virtue? Not to achieve or remain in power by flattering the crowd and aiming for public success, but to live according to the ideal of human excellence: putting the ideals of justice above all others. But how do we know what the criteria are for identifying these ideals? And what are the reasons why a virtuous action is superior to one that is not?

I believe that it is precisely in the question of the method chosen to defend the application and defense of ideals that all ethical philosophy can be understood. The discussion will not focus on the ethical principles selected as universal, but on the methods proposed to affirm or substantiate them.

Socrates, like many later authors (see the case of Professor Foerster cited by Max Weber as a representative of Catholic ethics), associates the practice of evil with ignoring the good, since it is in the good that the source of virtuous norms of action resides. The method for achieving this end is based on knowledge. Through self-knowledge and by teaching others how to carry out this self-examination (directed questioning in which the techniques of irony and maieutics are used), they will set themselves the task of understanding what is just or unjust, preferring just action to unjust action. Socrates proposes the formation of individual character as a mission in life, not as an area of interest only to candidates for public office, but as a prerogative for any well-lived human life.

---

[75] Plato, *Criton*, 48b, INIC, 1984, p.76

Socrates knew that for the political man this mission of self-discovery would become a difficult practice, because he also argued that it was the intrinsic nature of political power to be seduced by the honors and money that come with exercising it. So what connection is there with ethics? The (ideal) ruler would now have at his disposal the proposal of a practical method that would allow him to update his practice with the idea of virtue. He had a choice between the various pedagogical models of character formation, and for the first time he was aware of the tension between the pressure of the ideal and reality, between the interior and the exterior. What for? To fully realize his abilities as a rational being. What for? Just to be an enlightened citizen? Is this benefit seductive enough for the common man?

In a democracy, the education of rulers requires other ways of being carried out compared to what happens in tyrannies. The way in which the ruler is educated is defined by the philosopher Socrates, but the assumption that the politician is the philosopher is clearly made by Plato. Socrates proposed a system of rules of conduct for citizens, arguing that it was through knowledge that the individual could improve morally, but he didn't advocate any particular regime, nor did he propose a program for rulers in particular. However, we know that the aim of the ruler should be to make his actions fairer and to enhance this fairness in the relations between the citizens and each other, and between the citizens and the state.

When Plato[76] argues that it would be up to the "philosopher-king" to govern the city, he is not only proposing a pertinent method of forming the ruling classes in a democratic society, as opposed to the pedagogical method of the elites proposed by the Sophists, he is clearly indicating what the values should be that any human community should pursue at any time. The politician would be the philosopher in action. And reality to be transformed by the idea.

This clear struggle between the power of the philosophers, those who reflect on human action and interests in general, and the politicians, those who govern by extraordinarily conditioning human action in the name of localized interests, was not systematically a penalizing cause for the practical and current interests of peoples, it has to be said. Not least because, as we have already mentioned, Plato himself overcame this rigid separation between how societies should be and the philosophical interest in society as it is, in his book *The Laws*, and many philosophers ended up wanting to explain and identify methods of resolving concrete conflicts of action, rather than creating possible

[76] Plato, *The Republic*, Gulbenkian Publishing, Lisbon.

worlds.

For their part, politicians will always be on guard against the work and behavior of philosophers. But one fact is inescapable: the domains of politics and ethics will never cease to gravitate towards each other, either by open conflict, by avoiding interference, by ignoring each other in turn, or by devising strategies of adaptation. But the different positions occupied throughout history by the two spheres of action cannot be listed in one article, so here we'll just highlight a few moments along the way and try to outline schematically some proposals about the horizons of human action that both activities can offer us, just as the title of the article suggests.

Max Weber (1919) is the authority named by all those who question the link between the spheres of politics and ethics. In fact, Weber, in the text of one of his lectures, "Politics as a vocation", defends the fact that there is such a link, although he believes that there is a need to introduce a distinction in the meaning of ethics in order to be able to defend its relationship to political action, thus separating the "ethics of conviction" from the "ethics of responsibility". By the ethics of conviction he means the ethics of the ultimate ends themselves, for which the consequences of the intention, if put into practice, are not weighed up. The ethics of responsibility, on the other hand, implies accountability for the consequences of one's intentions, which could actually be foreseen in the actions taken.

For example, we can foresee the mathematical effects of a "benevolent intention" and take responsibility for them, not blaming them on some external force that we claim to be powerless to intervene against. With the ethics of responsibility, we assume that we are thinking about the foreseeable consequences of our decisions, and weighing up the value of our initial intentions against what they might cause. He recognizes that the relationship between the plane of intentions and that of actions is paradoxical, in the sense that the former aims at an individual work of perfecting character, or at defending an absolute demand for virtue as it is firmly understood by its author.

On the other hand, the plan of actions taken responsibly responds to the need to govern with the conditions of the present, adapting to the existing means and the possibilities arising from the historical situation in which individuals are integrated. The lack of openness to the consideration of error, and the idea that the idea of the good in itself justifies all action taken in its name, leads the author to draw attention to the danger associated with the defense of political action resulting from the pronouncement of the ethics of conviction.

At the end of the first decade of the 20th century, Weber called for an ethic of individual responsibility. [77]Weber called for an ethic of individual responsibility in order to avoid deluding or even confusing reality with an absolute idea of it. Weber notes that "The adherent of the ethics of conviction cannot stand the ethical irrationality of the world."[78]

I ask myself, does the adherent of the ethics of responsibility live up to the world as it is, just because it seems to react to the contingencies of history? Does accepting the ethical irrationality of the world as inevitable make actions better, and help to create better regulatory systems? Is there nothing left of the conviction that can be worked on in daily practice, updating the circumstances? The author admits that it is indeed possible to establish the two ethics as guides to political action. That's why he concludes that the complete political man is structured by the two, in unison.

If responsibility could never go hand in hand with conviction, Eleanor Roosevelt, the staunch defender of absolute and universal principles of human rights, would not have said that the easiest part of the whole process was to have them proclaimed by the United Nations General Assembly in 1945, in the form of a Universal Declaration, as this was the beginning of a long and arduous task for legislators and jurists around the world: That of gradually integrating these values into their political programs, first, then into the legislations of each nation, and finally disseminated.

The transition from ethical norms to customary norms of national and international law was taking place through politics, and over a much longer period of time than the convinced defenders of the theory had hoped. Today we know that this process of spreading, implementing and defending the instruments that would make the practice effective is far from over, as it continues to be criticized and corrected by each state, if not rejected by communities that characterize it as a standardizing document based on Western values that are said to be universal. Once again, we have here a struggle for the power to "educate" values to the people of the respective "cities", as if there were values that only belong to certain groups and with which they gain autonomy, independence and control. Who wins in the war of spreading values, does political power win?

Max Weber's horizon for discussion was the ongoing process of creating a state through revolution. The future Soviet state was being built on the basis of the

---

77 Proponents of cultural relativism often fall into this paradox. They argue that all cultures have the same value and should deserve equal respect, with the self-determination of peoples being a higher value, deserving an evaluation that does not make use of absolute value standards, most often Western standards. So, do we have to be tolerant of practices of excision because this is a cultural tradition, for example?

78 Max Weber, "Politics as a vocation", in *Tres tipos de poder e outros escritos,* ed. Tribuna, 2005, p.109.

convictions of a group of individuals, whose ends were evoked to justify the means used to achieve them. These were convictions that brought a theoretical conception that was intended to transform reality into practice. Karl Marx and Engels, the theoreticians, forced a philosophical turn from ethics when they criticized the contemplative tendency of all the philosophy that preceded them for its practical inconsequence. In this criticism, they even included the materialist Feurbach, because, according to them, even he had ended up incurring this common fault, that of abstracting reality, taking it to be an eternal state of affairs in its happening, refusing to consider the social conditions of each era.[79] We know that they are unfair in their criticism, as we saw in the example of Plato, and not only that, because if there is a fertile field for this extension of theory through practice, it is modernity, but knowing today the result of many rational and well-founded political proposals, do we really still defend the defense of ideals despite reality?

Max Weber knows that men fight for the impossible in order to achieve what is possible, but he also knows that action dominated by convictions, whose authors disregard the resistance of the governed or their opponents, can have extreme social repercussions, leading to war, extermination and absolute suffering. Taking resistance to the proposed measures as the fruit of ignorance or stupidity, which must necessarily be eradicated by all means in order to achieve the perfection of the model of conviction followed, thus disregarding the consequences of their action and provided that the designs of the political program are fulfilled, could open the door to all political arbitrariness and sectarian violence.

In the name of rational action, there is a danger of committing irrational actions. History has confirmed the destructive force of these new emerging political powers, supported by an ethics of conviction, assumed by young politicians who believed in their task of creating a more equal world in the name of the real freedom that the thinker had proposed as a goal.

Starting from the desire to change society and assuming that its foundations were the economic structures, with work as the element that creates social identity, then, by eliminating the division of labor, he would transform capitalist society into a classless system. In this society, it was imagined that there would be no place for repressive systems or social conflicts. All that was needed for this, according to Marxist theorists,

---

[79] Karl Marx, Engels, "A ideologia alema", *Works by Marx and Engels,* Lisbon, Avante.

"2. Critique of Feuerbach's contemplative and inconsequential materialism"; "(...) real liberation cannot be achieved except in the real world and with real means. (...) Communism is not for us a *state of affairs* that must be established, an *ideal* by which reality [must] regulate itself. We call communism the *real* movement that overcomes the current state of affairs."

was a massive transformation of all people, achieved through the revolutionary movement. The revolution would allow the definitive elimination of the ruling class in order to found a new classless society. The results were tragic for thousands of human beings.

At the same time, Weber is speaking to an audience of young Germans who have just emerged from the defeat of the Great War, not yet aware that it was only the first. Young people concerned with how to rebuild their state, without being dominated by resentment towards their leaders and foreign governments. We know that Weber did not succeed in his propaedeutic link to the creation of a democratic society. The German people were moving towards deepening their resentment and would soon have those who echoed their feelings of humiliation and non-conformity with the conditions of capitulation in their speeches. The results were tragic for millions of human beings.

Historically, Weber's work reflects the fact that there are citizens of a state who fight against it in order to create a new state, and it also reflects on the way out of a situation of world conflict involving states against states. These were the paradigms of political action in his decade: politics in its most violent form of imposing new orders. Politics as a means of exercising violence in a legitimate way, materialized in the acceptance of what was, or was not, in the interests of the state, as Max Weber concluded, by force of his historical circumstances.

But who is his intellectual adversary? He doesn't say so explicitly in his text, although he refers in passing to the philosophers of Christian ethics. However, we can think of all those philosophers who defend the primacy of normative principles as ultimate ends.

Three clear lines of research in ethics can be highlighted: 1. Ethics as a *corpus* of identified norms and principles, which aims to influence human action, conditioning it or aiming to determine actions to the ultimate ends of ethics in the name of the good life - teleology (and the history of the theory of the good from classical antiquity, through the ethics of life to utilitarianism, for example[80]); 2. Ethics as a method of rational justification/legitimization of guiding principles of conduct[81] - deontology (and its history linked to the theory of duty, since Kant); 3. Procedural ethics, which seeks to reconcile the cognitive formalism of deontological ethics with the question of intentions and their consequences, objectives, means used and practical consequences, with the aim

[80] One work that looks for regularities and similarities in the history of moral philosophy, as opposed to others that emphasize the differences, is Alain Caille's *Historia Critica da Filosofia Moral e Politica*, Verbo.

[81] Henry Sidgwick (1874), *Methods of Ethics,* Macmillan, London.

of overcoming the dichotomy between reason and sensibility, between acting out of duty and acting out of interest in a given good.

This text will now focus on the tests proposed by authors from this latter line of research, highlighting some of these working methods and focusing on the relationship between ethics and politics.

When it comes to ethical questions, isn't the focus of analysis on method, to the detriment of considering the formation of personal character and forms of social life that promote well-being in concrete terms, promoting abstract formalism? In a way, yes. This was the criticism of all the authors since Hegel who wanted to distance themselves from Immanuel Kant's initiative, claiming that he focused excessively on the rational justification of norms, neglecting the question of application, i.*e.* that he achieved the universal justification of norms without taking care of the particular issues related to the individual search for a good life, neglecting to investigate the socio-historical conditions that conditioned human action.

In his critique of Kant's philosophy, Hegel sought to identify the manifestations of morality in the concrete institutions that make up the political community, such as the state, civil society and the family, taking history as the link between ethical theory and moral practice, in order to explain his concept of "ethical life".

Kant sought to outline an answer to the question "What should I do?" For this author, the ultimate good of human action, defended since Plato and Aristotle as being the happiness of the individual and the social group, did not serve as the foundation of morality. He didn't recognize happiness as a sufficient cause for human beings to act morally. He sees happiness as something external to reason, unlike all the classical authors who identified happiness as deriving from the very exercise of rational activity. Starting from an analysis of the human faculties demonstrated in his practical and theoretical life, Kant will identify the one that everyone has in common, reason. And in this he was in agreement with his predecessors. This faculty serves to acquire knowledge but also to guide actions.

When reason tells us how to act, it manifests itself in the form of our moral conscience - practical reason. This conscience is only revealed because human beings have moral autonomy and can make their own choices, they have a free will. But this free will can lead them to act according to personal inclinations that have nothing to do with ethics. Kant gives us the famous example of the moral conscience of the shopkeeper who acts in an honest and socially correct way, being considered a man who acts well and aims for his own happiness, but with the aim of not losing the customer or his profit. For Kant, this is not a moral action.

In order for the ability to choose that man exercises through his will to be moral, Kant states that one cannot give in to external influences other than those associated with a good will, one that complies with the rule of always acting out of duty, keeping away the seduction of other interests and inclinations that could clash with man's ability to perfect his will. In other words, you should live according to your moral duty, without thinking about the consequences. And how do you know what your moral duty is? It's that which, at the moment the intention to act is formed, is established in accordance with the commands that your reason dictates to you. Commandments that will be presented as universal rules of procedure for any decisions that have to be made, for deliberations or actions to be adopted.

The commandments are presented in the form of categorical imperatives and appear in the following three types of formulation, as being a priori, necessary, universal and absolute: 1. "Act only according to a maxim such that you can at the same time want it to become universal law."; 2. "Act in such a way that you use your humanity, both in your own person and in the person of anyone else, always and simultaneously as an end and never simply as a means."; 3. "(Act) in such a way that the will by its maxim can consider itself at the same time as a universal legislator."[82]

Two centuries later, John Rawls continued along Kant's path and explored human moral capacity, trying to identify the set of principles that help us to make judgments or take actions that have what he calls a "sense of social justice". Twenty-five centuries later, Rawls' research continues along the lines of the movement begun in classical antiquity: to identify universal principles that are not subject to social pressures or political negotiations. The philosopher Rawls states[83] that justice is the highest virtue of a society's political and judicial institutions. In other words, they guide actions, define what is morally relevant and indicate priorities whenever there are disputes in society.

Rawls presents an interesting method to help define what he believes to be the greatest goal of all society: to define what a just action is, in order to be able to act and live in a system of social cooperation, regulated by justly chosen principles. The author tells us about the possibility of deliberating in an entirely free and equal way, as long as all those who hold representative positions and need to make decisions agree to carry out a thought experiment (a method of working in philosophy) which he calls the "idea of

[82] Immanuel Kant, *A metafisica dos costumes,* Lisbon, Presenga, pp. 59, 69, 76.
[83] John Rawls (1971), *A Theory of Justice,* Presenga, Lisbon.

the original position" - a pure procedural idea.

For Rawls, egoism, the "dictatorship of the first person", is the main obstacle to managing a society. But if we want to resolve disagreements between the various agents in dispute because of egoism, and without using physical force or skill, how do we proceed? Rawls says that if we manage to nullify the effect of the contingencies that cause disagreements between people, such as awareness of their social position and personal benefits, we will have the answer to the problem. But how, without it entailing a revolution? Rawls tells us that one or more people can proceed, by simulation (through intellectual exercise), from a "re-positioning" of themselves in a position in which they had no knowledge of their place/position in society, or even what their static, physical, cognitive, philosophical, religious, political, ethical (unaware of their conception of the good), psychic, emotional, cultural and material attributes were. They would also have no information about the goals of their lives, nor would they have any knowledge about the society in which they were inserted or the conditions of their existence as a social person. In this position, and after being informed that they would have to live with the consequences of their choices of principles, Rawls believes that their deliberations would lead to a selection of non-negotiated, universal principles.[84]

This "\uu of ignorance" that each person would bring down on themselves would position them in the ideal way of making choices and taking positions that affect the collective (being impartial and equitable in the allocation of favors or in the application of limits to interests that conflict with the advantages of the group in general). These advantages are manifested in what the author claims are the primary social goods, which are present in all ethical and moral theories from contractualism (the principles of social choice are the subject of an original agreement) to utilitarianism (definition of good as the satisfaction of rational desire, which produces the maximum satisfaction, or the greatest amount of well-being). His theory of justice seeks to link the two currents.

The theory of justice as equity takes up some aspects of both theories, while rejecting many other elements. In the theory of justice, the concept of what is just precedes the concept of what is good, which is why it is understood that there are regulatory principles (convergence of judgments reflected in justice) for human action.

John Rawls, however, doesn't just want to present a method for choosing just principles as long as they are considered to be the object of unanimous agreement; he also wants to talk about the substance of the agreement itself. Rawls argues that in this

---

84 Idem, pp. 121-147.

original position, any individual would defend two principles of minimum justice: equal opportunities and equal distribution of income and wealth; and equal basic freedoms for all. Principle of Freedom and Principle of Equality. But this is for individual agents. And for rulers, how is that?

When he thinks of politics, the philosopher refers to that which takes place in a constitutional, representative democracy, and thus argues that the assessment of what a fair decision should be will be manifested in the laws of each state's constitution.

The choices of laws and procedures that regulate the social order will also have to refer to this initial moment, this moment of production of rules that guide political decisions, based on the method of the original position proposed by Rawls' theory. It is assumed that the use of this method, this process of deliberation and choice, allows for the production of fair and just laws, while recognizing that the production of laws and decisions are made in the light of what is allowed by the circumstances. It is therefore imperfect procedural justice. In other words, it doesn't ensure economic and social equality, and this inequality ends up affecting the equality of political representation - political power becomes unequal, claiming benefits for a certain group that has accessed it. Rawls defines his aim as "to establish an ideal system, by comparison with which we can set a standard for judging existing institutions and show what justifies departing from such a model".[85]

We can conclude that Rawls' general and universal principles of justice should be used as criteria to analyze the actions of politicians and the justifications they give for them, but also the general conception of justice as a model for producing principles of action to guide politics, moving away from the ethical problem of defining what is the ultimate good.

But does Rawls explain the reasons why human beings seek consensus by resorting to the original position? We don't think so. Rawls tells us that he starts from the following principle: all subjects who will experience the original position are rational. But he doesn't explain how rationality is accessed or developed in human beings. This leaves the door open to arbitrariness, which Rawls says is not part of the process of deliberation by consensus. Because we think that in the very constitution of rationality there are rules that are being forgotten and could serve to support this position of deliberation by consensus.

On the other hand, believing that the human rational faculty is in itself a cause for

[85] Idem, p. 185.

resolving conflicts is rather ambiguous. Rawls makes no proposal to explain why the human capacity to judge things as just or unjust is acquired at a certain point in an individual's development, and what reason can be identified to justify our wanting to act in accordance with this assessment, expecting the same from others. Which theory of the formation of rationality does this refer to? We are not told.

In 2004, I wrote a text[86] which defended precisely the thesis that the ethics of discussion developed in the 20th century by authors such as Apel, Habermas, Camps or Alexy, would allow a structural articulation between theory and practice, insofar as ethical norms were produced in a communicational context, and in a process, which was itself ethical normative, since all interpersonal communication requires action oriented towards intercomprehension. Thus, any ethical norm could only be produced and accepted if all those interested in or affected by the effects of that norm were able to take part in a discussion about the validity, fairness and veracity of that norm, freely and on equal terms with everyone else. The collective interest could be served by a certain norm to be established as a practice, provided that this norm was verified and accepted by all those who would suffer the effects of its application.

Based on anthropological assumptions such as: 1. human individuation happens through socialization and not through genetic determinism; 2. the individual's self-determination is formed in a communicational context; Jurgen Habermas establishes that the individual and the community are co-founders of each other's identity, and that the creation of this identity takes place through language. Now, the meaning of each act of language is only apprehended (and learned) if certain conditions that validate it are met, namely: truth, fairness and veracity. Two or more participants in a discussion have to recognize the language used, but they have to admit that whatever language is used, there are conditions and requirements for the validity of language acts that are universal and unconditional.

Realizing ideals such as freedom, equality or social justice requires historical conditions for producing and applying them in the form of laws, and this can only be done through politics. But the conditions that politics has for doing this may well be those that the ethics of communication proposes and which are based on deepening the practices of real democracy. It doesn't propose equality of material conditions, because as John Rawls taught us, the distribution of goods such as freedom, justice or equal

---

[86] Isabel Salema Morgado (2004), *Uma etica para a Politica*, Lisbon, ed. Piaget.

But as early as 1997, in my master's thesis, I defended an intrinsic link between the philosophy of communication, as Karl Otto Apel presented it, and political action.

opportunities may not be equal among all, as long as the most disadvantaged gain from this distributive inequality, but it does advocate equal access to the discussion that determines decision-making, on the part of all those affected by this deliberation.

So I may have to pay more money to those who research methods to combat mental illness, for example, as this will strengthen the will to work in an area that will have enormous benefits for the whole community. But in a community of speakers it is recognized that it is through language, in the first place, that one can evaluate the conditions of validity of a description of the objective world, but also express intentions that are related to the experiences that each one has lived and also establish interpersonal relationships, which are established within a normative framework.

You might think that the most disadvantaged would also gain from being represented by labor, social and political authorities. That the entry into the world of political decision-making of all the community's speakers would create such a noise that one always thinks of the revolutionary explosion and what it has caused in the past. But the philosophers of communicational ethics argue that norms of action will be electable as regulatory principles as long as they have been consensually accepted by all those interested in their application, in terms of an intersubjective discussion (language in its interactive function), responsibility for the consequences is recognized and accepted, and dissent or refusal to accept them, or to agree on the objectives, by one or more individuals is respected and integrated, without detriment to provisional final decision-making, for utilitarian purposes and immediate decision-making.

For the authors in question, as long as the condition for becoming just (having normative correctness) is not met, the discussion must continue until all those involved reach a consensus. It doesn't identify the content of the end itself, the matter of the consensus to be reached, nor the time it will take, nor does it state that rejection or contestation should be eliminated from the discussion, but rather that all decision-making and all conflict resolution involves language as a means of communicational interaction. And only in this context is it possible to distinguish what is or is not a justified response.

This response to the problem of political decision-making is not based on a model of rationality determined by the cultural context, nor on another model that takes conscience as a guarantee of values, through acceptance or convergence of positions taken, but on a third alternative that involves, in the light of the theory of meaning, understanding, but also producing, norms that regulate and structure action.

Now, any decision that implies participation in a moral argument presupposes argumentative discussion in a community of speakers (in the establishment of intersubjective agreements), so that these gain meaning and can claim validity. It follows from the use of language, through everyday communicational practices, that discursive pragmatic assumptions are recognized which are normative from the outset. In other words, the right to participate and the right to equal treatment must be recognized for all subjects who are part of the community of speakers. But why? What if it's up to me, a powerful me, to ignore, disinterest or simply exclude someone from that decision?

Our life experiences atomize us. The suffering and pain of someone we care about is not really shareable, no matter how much empathy we feel. Pain that stems from a painful emotional connection to someone else who is in danger or, in turn, in pain. Pain that is the result of a situation of rupture, abandonment or domination, or pain caused by conditions that are aggravated by their fragile physical or mental health.

We know that in ordinary circumstances, our solidarity has its limits, which are those of our own self-perseverance and balance. "Forget it," we say to those who are unable to do so. "Believe that it will get better," we say to those who want to stop suffering so that we can stop doing it too and carry on with our usual distractions. "Get used to it," we demand of those who go through long periods of nonconformity and settle into them, eventually uninstalling us from ourselves. "Don't talk about it any more," we say in every possible way when someone talks about the loss of someone else, once, and then again and again and again.

But the philosophers of communication ethics affirm that in the context of decision-making involving shared and common interests, within the framework of communication ethics, solidarity is not the result of an intention, a desire or a force of will. Solidarity materializes when it is sustained by the general process of communicative socialization, which is updated to a greater degree every time compliance with norms that generate well-being increases. The discursive universal principle (U) is the rule of argument that serves as a criterion for justifying a norm, namely that all those affected by it consider it to be "equally good", and this is done through real discussion, taking into account the historical circumstances that frame the action. The method of poetic orientation is a method proposed in the ethics of communication: the method of extended discursive consensus.

"From this perspective, the Categorical Imperative also needs to be reformulated in the sense proposed: "Instead of prescribing to everyone else as valid a maxim that I want to be a universal law, I have to present my maxim to everyone else for discursive examination of its claim to universality. The weight shifts from what each (individual) can want without contradiction as a universal law to what everyone wants by common consent to recognize as a universal norm"[87] , says Jurgen Habermas.

The strategy of subordinating, of disregarding different positions, of suspending the right to participate and discuss, does not nullify the existence of these communicational structures. The existence of lies as a communicational way of living political and social life does not mean that the truth does not exist.

---

[87] Jurgen Habermas, *Consciencia moral e agir comunicativo*, ed. tempo brasileiro, Rio de Janeiro, 1989, p. 88.

English translation: *Moral Consciousness and Communicative Action,* transl. C. Lenhardt and S. W. Nicholsen, Blackwell, Oxford, p.67

3 Conclusion

The main merit of ethics will be to contribute a method of analyzing actions that does not add confusion, promote illusions and substantiate ideological narratives subordinated to certain interest groups. If we can avoid the fallacies of authority and demonstrate the manipulative discursive tactics and falsehoods involved in the production of many norms, then ethics will serve as a promoter of a set of rules that will help in the analysis, production and legitimization, through testing, of normative theories.

We can think of these ethical guiding principles for political action with the same degree of operability and application as the principle of falsification is for the scientific method. This was also the case with scientific research at the time of Galileo, when he opposed the force of the description of natural reality as Aristotle had understood it to one based on real evidence of how it could be. Even against the dominant beliefs of his time.

Let ethics be a way of thinking about action, and not a *corpus* of ultimate values of action, and let politics be the last phase of this method, that of application and experimentation, with the safeguard that the agent must always take responsibility for the foreseeable consequences. But are we close enough to presenting a rigorous and consensual method to carry out this task? Aren't we defending methods that are the result of beliefs about the value of action, from a cultural perspective that is meant to be universal?

On the other hand, isn't this the same proposal that has been put forward as a de facto hypothesis throughout the history of thought, with the damaging consequences of proceeding in the name of ethics to reorganize social reality as an object of study in a laboratory, raising it either to a level of abstraction from reality that is unfeasible or to a radical transformation of it, at the cost of the life and dignity of every human being, in the name of ideas? Is it possible to propose a set of rules that leave room for the individual's self-determination and at the same time allow the various social motivations for action to be articulated?

Let's see, if the intentions and motivations of human action could be captured in a formula that described human action in a quantitative way, we wouldn't need ethics or politics, because we would be entirely governed by measurable, determined forces, whose causality was governed by laws that, once known, would explain all behavior. But while science has found some behavioral regularities in the way we socialize (just look at the experiments of psychologists like Asch and Solomon on conformism, for example), it hasn't found a law that deterministically explains action and predicts behavior, no matter how much algorithms can predict some of our choices.

In human life, the relationship between causes and effects is much more complex than linear. And the defense of the "behaviorist" theorists fell apart when we realized the extent to which mental processes influence our behaviors and actions, being themselves a manifestation of a set of random variables. But if that's the case, why do we think it's possible to find universal principles that regulate behavior and not argue that it's possible to find a general law that defines behavior? Why is it important to consider the influence of social life experiences and the physical environment on the formation of personality, and conversely to try to universalize action-regulating principles through ethics?

The question of free will is problematic, since analysis of reality does not demonstrate to the fullest that the principle of self-determination of human will is an inescapable fact. I can believe that the freedom to choose is always possible, because the framework of human motivations, from the need to satisfy oneself to the need to be accepted and recognized by a group, are not absolutely determinant of every action in itself and in any circumstance. In other words, I can surprise others and above all myself when, despite the constraints of my socialization, I make choices that are not predictable.

If we could predict human behavior like we predict a final effect that results from a chain of causes of a certain phenomenon, we would have general laws. An explanation for everyone that could be certified through experimentation. But is this a de facto judgment? Does it describe reality? We don't know. Does this mean that I defend cultural relativism as the only ethical principle, in which it is assumed that the intentions of action are always determined by the cultural constraints in each context of socialization? Or do I defend indeterminism, by hypothesis? I answer both questions in the negative. In fact, identifying patterns of production, reception and acceptance of values that are the reasons that lead people to act is not, in itself, the work of a philosopher researching ethics.

If the nature of ethical norms or political principles that guide human behavior is the result of circumstantial and contingent actions, then we will be left with an archaeology of knowledge to understand the past, sociological surveys and behavioral observations by psychologists to explain the present, or surveys to envision the future.

If this is the case, we will not be able to value actions or establish priorities, unless we do so on the assumption that we are looking at individual and/or collective history, comparing actions of the past (in political analysis) with those of the present, seeking hypotheses for a possible idea of the future (in political action). In order to do this, particular attention would be paid to the efforts applied to the means that induce decision-making, as well as explaining and inventorying the way in which the different resources applied to accessing and acquiring these means are socially distributed, which affect the model of society in which each individual is integrated.

Resources such as intra-personal and social communication systems, the management of advertising or political campaigns, the study of the production process of cultural media, and the analysis of the means used for dissemination as well as the behaviors related to the reception of content by different audiences, passing through the exegesis of the syllabus of teaching and teacher training models, deontological and religious norms, as well as the different legislative conceptions and judicial practices of the society under study. Could ethics be done with all this?

Between the paradigm of the sciences of the psyche, that of the natural sciences and the ethnocentric and historical model of reality, is there no alternative to explain human action? Can't we propose futures? History on the one hand, science on the other? On the one hand the description of culturally adopted values, and on the other the factual description of reality. Is that all we have left as methods of analysis for human action?

The theory of argumentative communication sought to provide an operative answer to this question. In the long chain of solutions to the problem, this theory can be considered just another level in the search for truth, or it can be understood as the best intellectual effort we have to work on the issues of legitimizing public decisions and imposing social orders.

But isn't it absolutely appropriate to stick to the study of reality as it is experienced and perceived? Wouldn't a correct understanding of the circumstances that shape political action be expected to be substantially related to an adequate study of the means of social influence, as well as the way in which forces are produced that promote attitudes of conformism or adherence to certain model behaviors? Isn't it more scientifically rigorous to study the methods of selecting values and the human motivation for adherence or consent to them? This is if we want to reflect on the ethical and political issues linked to the dimension of human duty to be/duty to act.

So it's no more debauchery, no more real, that we suspend self-interest and examine the limitations and power of people and institutions in each period of time that each generation of individuals is given to live, and evil or good, unjust or just, truth or falsehood, are identified, defended, transformed, accepted or reused by each generation, in turn, within a legal framework for the defense of rights?

It is following scientific models that in the sëc. XX we investigate the socio-economic conditions of our time and present the data and analysis publicly, so that the public can make their own choices and have reasons or take advice on their own educational process. From this point of view, deliberately avoiding the defense of assumptions that prejudge the future based on a supra-historical idea that someone has of reality seems to be a designation for social ideas.

Hence the advocacy by some American theorists of a constitution that was minimalist from a substantive point of view, so that future generations could choose the answers they wanted within a reduced formal framework. But is this work enough to understand the dynamics of the formation and transmission of values? If so, how can we create political horizons, theories, beyond what can be achieved by comparison? And what is the legitimacy of these ethical-political proposals?

Does ethics propose horizons for human action, which would then become regular politics? The title of the article seems to suggest this, and in fact this ambiguity has materialized throughout history, on the assumption that ethics would be responsible for evaluating, and above all, explicitly indicating which values would (or should) be defended by political action. In this article, we set out to present a position that is legitimate to the idea that ethics should present itself as an activity that should substantiate and define the ultimate ends of human action.

The role of ethics as a working method for politicians and as a practical regulator of political action was defended, in line with research carried out in the philosophy of communication.

The emergence of ethics as a theoretical activity that allowed the presentation of norms to guide behavior, norms that resulted from a supra-historical, privileged view, did not prevent the emergence of intense conflicts that caused suffering to peoples throughout history, under the assumption that this was being done in the name of a higher good.

Assuming that ethics is more than an explanatory and critical action on the normative principles of human action and, eventually, a frame of reference for the values derived from political action, we can understand the reaction of opposition to the hypothesis that through ethics we are able to define the ultimate ends that should guide human existence. Understanding ethics as an intellectual activity through which norms are produced that can be imposed on communities through politics, assisted by the judiciary in modern states, is a reckless and risky position.

Any historian will show you the events and the serious social implications of misunderstanding the relationship between ethics and politics over time. Ethical philosophers, in wanting to present their theories as being based on the universal and superior ability of human reason to search for foundations, validate norms and propose guidelines, as opposed to the set of norms derived from social pressure groups or other belief systems, such as religious ones, have not failed to incur errors of legitimization and application.

And it is incomparably less incisive to criticize these theories for being non-commensurable theories about human reality (because that would be a very pertinent problem, but in the order of scientific criticism) than it is to criticize them for being conducive to the application of political systems that have subjected societies to endless iniquities.

Does refusing to make a history of the relationship between the fields of ethics and politics, because we reject the hypothesis of the evolution of systems in history, allow us to better explain and understand our social reality? Is this break between the narratives and theories that regulate action in the present and those that regulated action in the past more coherent from the point of view of creating solutions to current conflicts?

Does saying that all the so-called stages of historical development are random and without any identified meaning allow us to reflect more theoretically on the origin, nature and purpose of human action? Defending it would be like defending, as Thomas Kuhn did for the natural sciences, and the post-modernists did for the social sciences, that there is no truth. Nor justice. Nor meaning.

The danger in accepting or defending ultimate values is, as Victoria Camps[88] warns us, the dangerous preponderance of those who claim for themselves, or who are claimed by others, as "guardians of norms". This results from the appropriation that other personalities can make of good values. What ethics will have to offer is a working method that operates, without submitting, to the arbitrariness of powers - so that it isn't used to serve group political interests that bring more injustice, perversity and suffering. But ethics is also expected not to evade the need to contemplate the contradictions of the agents involved in the decisions and choices of public life, and not to guide them towards practices they refuse or don't understand. It is this point of balance that is sought.

---

[88] Camps, Vitoria (1983), *Etica, retdrica, politico*, Madrid, ed. Alianza Universidad.

However, we have to analyze the mistakes that were made when theories were proposed to substantiate principles, as opposed to the advantages of theories that indicate formal guidelines or procedures. We want ethical statements to be methodological in nature, leaving politics with the task of updating them and using them to propose measures or actions that regulate behavior according to a universal principle of action. The problem is that we can't test for error.

I can't look for mistakes when I make political proposals, because people shouldn't be used as experimental animals in laboratories. Social experiments with economic theories, which cause serious and permanent ruptures with the way of life we want socially, conform to a non-violent and disorderly model of existing in society. Let's not just talk about the thousands of deaths that are drowned out by these waves of social experiments (but let's not forget them, ever), let's talk about the subjugated, humiliated and disbelieving lives that survive.

Through ethical reflection, measures can be implemented that can be measured, leaving politics to update and substantiate itself historically. Each historical period solves problems with the concepts and solutions that each group finds for the moment, allowing for creativity, innovation and uncrystallized development, albeit within a framework of ethical-normative references that can hopefully be universal. Proposals of values with a list that culminates in the presentation of an ultimate value in itself, allows for the greatest political follies in the name of the idea of good, justice, dignity, freedom, in short.

If we assume a dictum that identifies absolute values, we always run the risk of not listing enough intangible values that would be subsidized by irrevocable rights in the first place. The list may fall short of what is socially desirable. Secondly, an individual or a group can claim the configuration of this right within the framework of their own understanding of it, and propose it as the final solution.

Values, rules, guidelines, lists of duties, charters, constitutions, declarations of principles, regulations are, if they claim to be universalist, proof of the struggle between what human thought thinks is possible and what individual human action realizes is applicable.

Reflecting on the question of ethics and politics as a guiding structure that looks at the present and places us in some preferential historical horizon, with well-explored and assumed consequences, gives us the temporal dimension of the future expected or longed for by a given generation, of a given culture, and is based on the ancient idea that a well-justified theoretical ideal should guide practice, rather than merely describing or explaining it.

We are not told how to act, but what are the best and most justified means we have at present to help us decide how to act within the framework of rational action - that is, action that can present good reasons to justify it, i.e. that stand up to scrutiny and are accepted by the community on the basis of the search for mutual understanding. To deepen a common life that doesn't lead to mutual destruction. How long can apathy or indifference last in the face of arbitrary command or the defense of private interests over those of the community?

What is this revolution of 2017 that in some countries has materialized in the use of images and posters, language and attacks of extreme violence against the integrity of the character of opponents? Why are they listened to? Who listens to them? I think this message has been circulating for a long time. And not so suddenly... it became acceptable.

Apel, Karl-Otto (1991), "Is the ethics of the ideal communication community a utopia? On the relationship between ethics, utopia, and the critique of utopia", In *The Communicative Ethics Controversy,* (edit.) Seyla Benhabib and Fred Dallmayr, Massachusetts and London, MIT Press.

Apel, Karl-Otto (1991), *Teoria de la Verdady Etica del Discurso,* transl. Norberto Smilg, Barcelona, Paidos.

Aristotle, *Politics,* translated by A. Amaral and C. Gomes, Lisbon, Veja.

Aristotle, *Nicomachean Ethics,* transl. Antonio Caeiro, Lisbon, Quetzal editores.

Blackburn, Simon, "How is analytic philosophy possible?", http://ateus.net/artigos/filosofia/como-e-a-filosofia-analitica-possivel/,consultado on September 28, 2012.

Cailld, Alian and others (2001), *Historia da Critica da Filosofia Moral e Politica,* transl. Antonio Campleo Amaral and others, Lisbon, Verbo.

Habermas, Jurgen (1981), *Theorie des kommunikativen Handelns*, vol.1 and 2, Suhrkamp, Frankfurt, 1985. English transl. English translation: Jurgen Habermas, *The theory of Communicative Action,* vol 1 and 2, transl. Thomas McCarty, Polity press, 1987. French translation: Jurgen Habermas, *Theorie de Tagir communicationnel*, vol.1e2 trad. Jean-Marc Ferry, Paris, ed. Fayard.

Habermas, Jurgen (1999), "From Hegel to Kant and Back again: The Move towards Detranscendentalization", *European Journal of Philosophy* 7 (2), August: 129-157.

Habermas, Jurgen *(1983), Moralbewusstsein und Kommunikatives Handeln.* Portuguese translation: *Consciencia Moral e Agir Comunicativo*, ed. Tempo brasileiro, Rio de Janeiro, 1989. English translation: *Moral Consciousness and Communicative Action,* Oxford, Polity Press.

Hare, R. M., (1981), *Moral Thinking: Its Levels, Method, and Point,* Oxford, Clarendon Press.

Hegel, Georg, (1837), *La raison dans l'histoire*, Paris, Librairie Plon.
(Trad. Portuguese at: http://pt.scribd.com/doc/7216150/Hegel-A-Razao-Na-Historia)

Jaeger, Werner, (1979), *Paideia*, trad. Artur M. Parreira, Aster editorial.

Kant, Immanuel (1785), *Grundlegung zur Metaphysik der Sitten.* Portuguese translation: *Fundamentaqao Metafisica dos Costumes*, transl. Paulo Quintela, Lisbon, Edicoes 70, 1995.

Kant, Immanuel (1788), *Kritik der praktischen Vernunft.* Portuguese translation: *A Critica da Razao Pratica,* trad. Artur Morao, Lisbon, ed. 70, , 1994.

Macintyre, Alasdair (1994), *After Virtue, A Study in Moral Theory*, London, Duckworth.

Macintyre, Alasdair (1998), *A Short History of Ethics,* Notre Dame, Indiana.

Mill, John Stuart (1863), Utilitarianism, http://www.utilitarianism.com/mill1.htm, consulted in July 2012.

Marx, Karl and Engels, Friedrich (1845), "The German Ideology", ch. 1, *Marx and Engels - Selected Works,* Lisbon, Avante.

Marx, Karl, (1845) "Theses on Feuerbach", *Marx and Engels - Selected Works,* Lisbon, Avante.

Platao, *Apologia de Socrates*, transl. Manuel Pulqudrio, Lisbon, INIC.

Platao, *A Republica*, trad. Mª helena Rocha Pereira,Lisboa, Gulbenkian.

Plato, *The Politician*, transl. Carmen Soares, Lisbon, Circulo de Leitores.

Platao, *Leis,* transl. Carlos Humberto Gomes, Belem, UFPA.

Plato, The *Seventh Letter,* Trad. Trindade dos Santos and others, Rio de Janeiro, Ed. PUC and ed. Loyola

Rawls, John (1982), *Sobre las libertades*, transl. J.V. Rubio, Barcelona, ed. Paidos.

Rawls, John (1971), *Uma teoria da Justiga*, transl. C. P. Correia, Lisbon, Ed. Presenga.

Singer, M. G. (1971), *Generalization in Ethics*, New York, Macmillan Public.

Talbott, William J., (2005), *Which rights should be universal?,* New York, Univ. Press

Williams, Bernard (1993), *Ethics and the Limits of Philosophy,* London, Fontana Press.

Weber, Max (1919), "A política como vocação*, Tres tipos de poder e outros escritos,* Lisbon, Tribuna, pp. 63-115.

Winch, Peter (1972), *Ethics and Action,* London, Routledge & Kegan Paul.

Printed by Books on Demand GmbH, Norderstedt / Germany